TOTAL COST OF OWNERSHIP IN MANUFACTURING INDUSTRY – BASICS AND MORE

PETRI S. NIEMINEN

0   FOREWORD

"Can't see the forest but only the trees" is a fluent translation of a Finnish saying "Ei näe metsää puilta", which basically means that one can see only the single units, the trees, but not the whole entity that is the whole forest including trees together, undergrowth, flowers and other small plants growing and many kinds of animals living in the forest.

The same can be applied in business in any working position: We can see the elements but not the big picture. Because of this, we make our decisions based on partial information about the whole truth, which then leads to not comprehensively understanding the business-related consequences of the decisions made. For example, making an investment decision based on the lowest procurement price, leading to a saving of 20 000 € upon the initial purchase increasing the operating or maintenance expenses worth of 0,2 € per product in the lifetime volume of 7 years of production with total volume of 400 000 pieces. This means that the 20 000 € saving on the initial price ends up costing 80 000 € in operational expenses. As a result, we easily end up wondering why total expenses keep on increasing despite putting so much effort into saving on the initial purchase price.

And this is where the concept called Total Cost of Ownership, TCO, steps in. As the name very well describes, it is a concept focusing on defining all the aspects of all costs related to a purchase. Moreover, it can be applied to working processes and anything in business and many things, also in private life. Furthermore, by optimizing total costs of ownership, much more sustainable financial gains can be made than, for example, the temporary savings achieved by laying people off in an economic downturn. And this is exactly what makes TCO such a versatile tool in trying to make more money in business.

It is also one reason this book exists: To try to convince decision makers in business life that there are many more ways to make money in business than just trying to buy low, sell high and lay off a lot of the personnel during the first financial hiccup. But more about this in the later chapters of this book.

In this book, to make it efficient just like the concept itself, Total Cost of Ownership is referred to as TCO. Based on research done on the topic during the writing process of this book, TCO is the common abbreviation, which means it can be used in any aspect of the whole concept if wanting to search for further knowledge beyond what's written in this book. As an author, I also do not claim to know everything about TCO. Just like you, the reader of this book, I am also a student of this topic, even if I already know quite a bit. And I've also brought my experience into the creation of this book, often referred to as "(author's experience)" to distinguish it from the information or ways of expressing things coming from other sources. I also want to make a notion that this is not a 100% schoolbook. Aside from bringing in my knowledge of Total Cost of Ownership that I already have plus what I learn in the process of making this book, I also intend to bring in my motivations for the whole topic, which can be seen in a few parts of this book, remarked as "(author's view)". I find it highly fascinating to learn new aspects of the topics I am interested in. And you, the reader, also have complete freedom to apply anything you find useful within this book in your own private life or in business. However, I strongly recommend reflecting it in the conditions under which these things are being applied, such as data systems available, corporate culture, strategy and so on to achieve actual financial gains. A single universal model of TCO that works everywhere equally well does not exist.

However, at this point I want to apologise for not having any pictures in this book. My intention was to have quite a few pictures, but life and general terms and conditions got in the way. And I don't intend this as blame; it is what it is. I hope this will not hinder your motivation to get to know this fascinating subject.

Without further ado, let us embark on a fascinating journey on the comprehensive ship that is called TCO and sail the seas of complex interdependencies and waves of decision making.

Sail on!

Abbreviations & Glossary

TCO = Total Cost of Ownership

KPI = Key Performance Indicator

OPEX = Operation Expense

CAPEX = Capital Expenditure

OEM = Original Equipment Manufacturer

Cost from the supplier's point of view = The price it pays to its own suppliers for goods or services and what it pays to internal/external personnel for the related work to implement the goods/services.

Price from the supplier's point of view = Cost + profit margin (+ contingency).

Initial cost = The price tag including the full cost breakdown + the internal work gone into getting the quotations + work done until before installation and commissioning.

Cost of operation = All costs during installation and commissioning phase, including related tests and test material, internal work of potential issue resolution and quality development. This also includes the energy and process utility consumption of a piece of physical machinery.

Cost of maintenance = All costs related to preventive, documenting and reactive maintenance of the purchase item.

Cost of downtime = All costs related to the stoppage of work because of malfunction or failure of the purchased item.

Cost of production = Capacity, availability, quality output and environmental impact of the purchase item, as well as potential rework and scrapping costs related to quality defects.

Remaining value / Costs of disposal = What is the total cost effect of the end of the planned use life of the purchase item? Can it be, e.g. sold onwards or reused?

CBD = Cost Breakdown = Splitting the total quotation over several items, showing the total € for each item separately.

MTTR = Mean Time To Repair

MCTR = Mean Cost To Repair

NPD = New Product Development

NDA = Non-disclosure agreement

CoP = Community of Practice

SoP = Start of Production

Table of Contents

PART A – BASICS, APPLICATIONS AND IMPLEMENTATION OF TCO

Even though many aspects of Total Cost of Ownership are considered at work, and thought of, for example, during the purchasing process, they're mostly not considered as one connected concept. Just like one of our managers said when I was holding a TCO basic training at work, "This concept gives a clear structure to all these topics".

Just like with any big topic, we must start from the basics, starting with its importance and a practical real-life example to help you, dear reader, understand the topic. After this, we'll elaborate on the elements of TCO. And, even though these elements contain quite a bit to internalise, knowing the theory alone won't be very useful if not applying it, nor knowing how to apply it, which is why after going through the elements of TCO we shall look into how to apply and implement it. And to help the implementation, we must understand in which situations it can be applied, as well as certain basic terminology and concepts within cost engineering and management accounting. Let's not forget one of the key requirements for success at any transformation change in a working organisation, either: management commitment. After all, management is in a crucial position to ensure the workload, non-human resources and facilitation of collaboration to succeed at implementing the Total Cost of Ownership. Let's set our sails and embark our fascinating journey together.

1   BASICS OF TCO

" No gain is so certain as that which proceeds from the economical use of what you already have", says a Latin proverb (Forbes, 2015). The Latin language has a lot of proverbs that are simple yet contain a lot of truth within. In TCO, this exact proverb applies especially well, as it can be extended both to what we already have, and to what we are planning to achieve or obtain. And this is basically what TCO is all about: understanding the comprehensive view of the total costs related to any purchase item, asset, organisational function and so on. And when we understand the whole big picture, we can make better-informed decisions, which leads to improved operational efficiency and profitability.

Traditionally, TCO contains the following categories:

> initial cost

> cost of operation

> cost of maintenance

> cost of downtime

> cost of production and

> remaining value.

But there is much more to the whole concept, both in terms of cost elements included as well as time scope of each purchase topic. In fact, even though TCO is often considered to start from receiving the quotation for the requested goods or services and activities related to the selection of the supplier and the goods or services to be procured and making the purchase decision, a lot of effort is put into the topic in question already even long before the purchase decision is made. These cost components can be described as pre-transaction components, and they include, for example:

> identifying the purchase needs

> investigating and contacting potential suppliers for the needed goods or services

> checking the background and financial status of the suppliers

> mutual education for the supplier to get to know their customer and vice versa

> creating the technical specifications for the purposes of *Request for Quotation* and

> adding the selected supplier into the corporate data systems if required.

Next, in the chronological order of a purchase, are the transaction components. These are the cost elements related to the whole initial purchase itself, from the supplier selection all the way until the goods or services have been received, evaluated, verified OK and paid. These cost components include things like:

- ➢ purchase price
- ➢ preparation and placement of the purchase order
- ➢ follow-up and potential correction needs
- ➢ costs related to interim approvals if required
- ➢ delivery transportation
- ➢ tariffs and duties
- ➢ billing and payment
- ➢ inspection of the received goods or services
- ➢ (reclamation and related correction process)
- ➢ installation and commissioning in the case of physical goods
- ➢ required qualification or training.

Each of these cost components can and should also be evaluated separately, but this evaluation work is also part of the total cost of ownership of each purchase. Thus, I strongly recommend putting the most effort in the comparison of the major cost drivers, but light evaluation of even minor cost drivers is recommended, because it is not very uncommon to realize something particularly important for the whole purchase when analysing each cost component.

Lastly, there is the third category of cost components called post-transaction components. These include:

- ➢ line fallout = percentage of anticipated defects by Supplier for all parts and/or assemblies (Law Insider Inc., 2013-2024).
- ➢ defective finished goods rejected before sales
- ➢ preventive and reactive maintenance and related downtime
- ➢ customer goodwill
- ➢ potential reputation effects from good or bad punctuality and/or quality of delivery of products
- ➢ energy and water costs
- ➢ disposal costs at the end of the use life (Ellram, 1993).

This third category of cost components is in a way quite paradoxical. As it is often the most distant one from the purchase in time, it is least frequently considered in relation to a specific purchase. Yet, this category can form the biggest share of the overall TCO due to its long duration. This underlines the importance of Total Cost of Ownership further when comparing all expenses related to any purchase.

1.1 Why is TCO important

Total Cost of Ownership is highly beneficial when aiming for improved profitability in any area of business, any function or any activity. This boils back down to the Latin proverb presented at the beginning of this chapter. And thus, it doesn't apply only to purchasing and collaboration with suppliers but also many other aspects, such as internal working processes, quality, supporting business strategy work, evaluation of stakeholder value and making quotations for potential customers. This is because, as cynical or materialistic as it sounds, almost anything can be measured in money. And this is true even if not all costs can be allocated per purchase or asset and many things cannot be defined in money until being fully completed, seeing the total actualized costs. Furthermore, TCO helps in showing how all these are interconnected in business.

Moreover, where TCO also brings a huge added value is in planning work. This is because a proper TCO evaluation requires vast amounts of clarification, investigation and data if one wants to form a comprehensive picture of costs related to any purchase or process ownership. While conducting these clarifications and data collection, it often happens that some crucial points are realized and would have been missed without this work (Spencer, 2024). TCO plays a big role also in financial feasibility studies and financial decision making because by understanding the TCO of a single purchase and even an entire project, more accurate financial projections can be made about the expenses and returns in each case. Being applicable for entire projects means TCO is also a highly useful concept in program management, which, among other tasks in it, concerns prioritization of different projects and the resources between them (Fernandes. 2023).

A TCO model also benefits decision making and potentially gives a full indication of total costs and returns on investment of a purchase. Through this, maybe the option with the lowest purchase price will turn out expensive, for example, by significantly increasing handling and warehousing costs (Logistiikan maailma, 2024). Furthermore, Total Cost of Ownership is not only applicable in internal decision-making and internal processes but also in business-to-business trade and with suppliers and other external stakeholders. For example, many companies nowadays require a complete analysis of total cost of ownership from their suppliers to make more informed decisions in supplier selection and so on (Fishman Corporation, 2024). Besides this, TCO has plenty of other benefits and uses that are handled in this book. But enough theory for now; let us look at a real-life practical example.

Moreover, where TCO also brings a huge added value is in planning work. This is because a proper TCO evaluation requires vast amounts of clarification, investigation and data if one wants to form a comprehensive picture of costs related to any purchase or process ownership. While conducting these clarifications and data collection, it often happens that some crucial points are realized and would have been missed without this work (Spencer, 2024). TCO plays a big role also in financial feasibility studies and financial decision making because by understanding the TCO of a single purchase and even an entire project, more accurate financial projections can be made about the expenses and returns in each case. Being applicable for entire projects means TCO is also a highly useful concept in program management, which, among other tasks in it, concerns prioritization of different projects and the resources between them (Fernandes. 2023).

A TCO model also benefits decision making and potentially gives a full indication of total costs and returns on investment of a purchase. Through this, maybe the option with the lowest purchase price will turn out expensive, for example, by significantly increasing handling and warehousing costs (Logistiikan maailma, 2024). Furthermore, Total Cost of Ownership is not only applicable in internal decision-making and internal processes but also in business-to-business trade and with suppliers and other external stakeholders. For example, many companies nowadays require a complete analysis of total cost of ownership from their suppliers to make more informed decisions in supplier selection and so on (Fishman Corporation, 2024). Besides this, TCO has plenty of other benefits and uses that are handled in this book. But enough theory for now; let us look at a real-life practical example.

1.2   Practical example

Imagine you have decided to buy a car. For some of us this is exciting; for some of us this is stressful and just a necessary "evil" to make do in life without proper public transport or not to be tied to fixed schedules. Whichever is the case, I hope this example can be of some use. However, I recommend proceeding with caution in pairing this practical, non-corporate example to everyday life in business: Many aspects of a car might be more of a question of emotion to many of us, rather than sense, whereas I hope most of the decisions are made in business with logic and reason, rather than emotion. Therefore, we shall apply here what some call "cold business" and stick to the evaluation of total cost of ownership. And to avoid taking half the book with this example, we shall simplify.

When buying a car for everyday use, many of us start by pondering what kind of car it should be. And just like described in the opening chapter of this book, this is where the TCO starts, even though this phase applies to any of the options out of which one will ultimately be selected. However, even though the amount of work done, and time spent, at this phase might be quite similar regardless of which option we finally end up with, the decisions made at this point may have an enormous impact on the total cost of ownership of the car we ultimately end up choosing. Unless the choice is already obvious, many of us start with the body type of the car. Should it be a sedan, station wagon, hatchback or perhaps an SUV? All of them have their benefits and reasons why people tend to choose any of them, but with pure reason, this choice is often made based on the required amount and type of load capacity. Basically, this means how many people the car must transport around regularly and how much cargo besides people. Aside from the number of people, also their physical size matters; how big a car you need. From the point of view of total cost of ownership, I recommend keeping in mind that unnecessary weight and height increases the fuel costs, albeit there are many other factors that affect those, too.

Once the body type has been decided, it is time to evaluate what can be called the driving profile: How many kilometres or miles you drive annually on average and where do you drive? Is most driving done in a city or highway? Do you drive regularly on roads that are not in good condition? This information tends to be used to determine the best choice of fuel. In addition to the actual need, it's also important to keep the potential restrictions in mind. In this case, they might be fuel and size restrictions, for example, in some major cities. Also, not choosing a bigger engine than is really needed is often beneficial to the total cost of ownership of the car.

After this consideration has been done, the next one is to think about the budget of both the initial purchase, as well as operation costs. And this is where careful consideration is needed in the estimation between potential funding costs of a more expensive, newer car in comparison to an older and cheaper car potentially requiring more maintenance. Here, it's good to consider how much of the maintenance we can do ourselves; do we have a helpful family friend to assist us, or do we need to outsource all maintenance and repairs to a professional? And how often and how extensive maintenance might be required. Another very important aspect here is to do some research to find out what kind of common faults the vehicles we are considering have, how expensive those faults might be to repair and if they might put us in a risk of being left stranded on the side of the road, increasing the total cost of ownership by having to resort to a tow truck. The third aspect to consider here is the depreciation in value. Cars tend to lose 30-50% of their initial purchase value within the first 2-3 years of ownership and first 50 000 km or so of driving, which is something we should also consider in the total cost of ownership of a car. This, plus the fact that optional extras, meaning additional equipment on top of so-called baseline equipment, lose value, too. This means it is possible to purchase a 2–3-year-old car with more features cheaper than a brand new, less well-equipped car.

Next, we come to the insurance and taxation expenses. Depending on the national or regional legislation, these might depend even strongly on the engine size or the fuel type and fuel consumption of the car. The difference might be hundreds or even thousands of euros per year, which means this is a very considerable expense. And the fuel consumption can make an enormous difference in itself, depending on the fuel price and how much the average annual mileage is.

What we also should consider is how long we are planning to keep the car. This has a tremendous impact on the required longevity. We might plan to keep it only for a year or, for example, ten years. This also commonly influences whether we decide to go for a newer car with less mileage or an older car with often a cheaper purchase price.

Lastly, unless we are going to drive the same car for as long as it is economically viable to keep it going, we should consider the potential resale value. The longer we are planning to keep the car, the harder it will be to predict any trends affecting the resale value at the time, but what we can do is going for reputable brands with some features that have a positive impact on the resale value. In many cases, reputable brands also tend to build more reliable cars, but this cannot be taken for granted. It is better to resort to your own research on the exact type of vehicle you're looking for. Of course, another aspect affecting the resale value is how well we're going to take care of the car. If not even replacing the engine oil, or having it done by a professional garage, I would not worry about the resale value too much because a badly maintained car is hard to sell for anything near the average market value. Additionally, skipping the maintenance saves money only during the time of skipping the maintenance, but it increases the total cost of ownership later, sometimes even exponentially.

As a car enthusiast I could carry on about this topic for a whole week or maybe for a whole book, which I someday might, but since it's best spared for some other occasion, let's return to the topic at hand, the total cost of ownership and its elements.

1.3   Elements of TCO

As discussed in the opening chapter of this book, there are multiple ways to categorize TCO. In this book we shall follow the more traditional categorisation, which includes:

- ➢ initial purchase
- ➢ operation cost
- ➢ maintenance cost
- ➢ downtime cost, which is sometimes included within maintenance costs
- ➢ production cost and
- ➢ remaining value (Graco Inc., 2024).

This categorisation is selected because much of the literature on the topic seems to follow this, or a very similar categorisation, and because it helps to keep the categorisation clear. Furthermore, the topics discussed in the opening chapter of this book shall be included within this categorisation, since they are essential elements of total cost of ownership. However, there are other ways to categorize TCO, too, including examples related to each category:

- Initial purchase
  - o Purchase price including cost and supplier margin
- Cost incurred
  - o Transport and packaging
  - o Payment terms
  - o Customs duties
- Cost of acquisition
  - o Procurement department operations
- Cost of ownership
  - o Stock management
  - o Depreciation costs
- Cost of maintenance
  - o Spare parts
  - o Servicing

- Cost of usage
  - Use value
  - Operation
  - Services
- Cost of poor quality
  - Deadline compliance
  - Non-compliance process
- Cost of disposal
  - Recycling
  - Resale
  - Deconstruction (Manutan, 2024).

And this is an equally correct way to categorize TCO. In my experience, it's best to select a categorization that helps in paying attention to all relevant cost elements, given that all the related cost items are considered. This is crucial, because then we can avoid ending up having to wonder about hidden costs when analysing the development in financial performance. Another vital aspect of the whole TCO evaluation is to conduct a full analysis instead of doing it incrementally when each phase is occurring. If no cost data is available for one or more of these phases beforehand, it's still better to estimate rather than skip. This should be done to understand the full total cost of ownership proactively, because only then can it be used as a decision-making basis during the planning. That said, calculating TCO reactively can provide vital cost data and understanding of the overall cost structure of setting up and running a production line and disposing of it at the end of its use life. So, without further ado, let's start with what is usually the most recognized category, initial purchase.

1.3.1 Initial cost

The initial cost is the very price tag in the quotation requested for procuring the goods or services (Graco Inc., 2024). Depending on the complexity of the purchase in question, it might consist of several cost elements. For example, with industrial equipment, the quotation might contain cost elements such as project management or overheads, engineering or design, manufacturing of the equipment, delivery, installation and commissioning. Whether these cost elements, and, for example, initial on-site support, are included in the quotation, depends on the agreed delivery scope with the potential supplier.

But this is not where the total cost of ownership starts. As discussed in Chapter 1 of this book, the TCO starts from identifying the purchase need (Ellram, 1993). In essence, this means finding out what needs to be purchased to achieve the targeted result, for example, in a single process phase. Depending on the complexity of the topic at hand, this phase contains very different numbers of process steps. One of the simplest cases is, for example, a replacement investment in which the actual purchase is carried out to maintain the production output capacity that is lost through output decay and scrapping (Fedelstein & Rotschild, 1974). If other conditions or requirements haven't changed, pretty much all that is needed is a new piece of equipment very similar to the currently existing one. That said, even in this case, in many countries and regions it is mandatory to have a tendering process between potential suppliers for supplying the needed equipment. In practice, this means the potential suppliers are requested to send competing quotations for the needed equipment.

On the other hand, if the required item of goods or services is very complex, the phase of defining the purchase need can be quite extensive. For example, an entire set of similar types of process tooling with many differences between them often requires a lot of collaboration between the technical and the procurement personnel, as well as with potential suppliers. The latter might be the case, especially if the equipment or the whole technology behind it is very new to the company procuring it. And even though all this might sound like the amount of work done here is similar between different options of equipment, out of which we end up selecting only one, I strongly recommend considering this phase in the total cost of ownership, because the choices made in this, and other pre-transaction phases will affect the total cost of ownership of the equipment in question significantly. If the type of the equipment is very new to the company procuring it, based on my experience I recommend at this point to start contacting the potential suppliers very latest as soon as the potentially relevant supplier candidates have been mapped out to benefit from their expertise in the equipment selection, helping to optimise the total cost of ownership of the needed equipment.

If extensive clarifications are required in this phase, often the technical specifications for the required equipment or services are created at least partially in parallel with this work to fully determine the purchase need.

Creating thorough technical specifications increases the chances of success in any technical purchase. And not only during the purchase phase but also throughout the whole lifecycle of the entity that the purchase is related to, such as an entire production line (Cooper, 2020). The purpose of a technical specification can vary greatly depending on what it is intended for. It can be an accurate technical description of what is needed from a supplier containing for example a verbal description of the item needed, a description and layout of the production process where the item will be installed and utilized and accurate technical details of the item needed including for example measurements and tolerances, a 3D model and a simulation model (author's experience). Besides the technical part, the technical specifications must include also what work is involved concerning the item to be purchased, impact and the timeline of the project in which it's purchased (Cooper, 2020).

Successful creation of an accurate and clear technical specification is indeed vital to the success of a project and to its TCO due to several different benefits. One of the most immediate effects is that the more accurate, realistic and correct the specification documentation is, the easier it is for a supplier to give an initial pricing and delivery time that will hold all through the planning, execution, installation and commissioning phases. And not only does this happen by maximising the suppliers' chances of estimating the pricing and timing correctly but also since the more accurate, correct and realistic the specific documentation is, the less there is a risk for rework need by suppliers during design and manufacturing process. Additionally, the correctness and accuracy of the specification documentation will lead to reduced monitoring and follow-up needs during a design and manufacturing process, which frees up time for the personnel in the company ordering the purchase item to focus on other work. Directly this saves working hours in the total workload towards the personnel engaged in ordering and following up the planning and execution of the purchase item and indirectly it reduces stress and risk of making mistakes from having so many topics to work on, which reduces the error risk in other work. All this has a great chance of leading to further cost savings both directly through saved working hours and improved quality of work and further indirectly by improving customer satisfaction through improved quality and timeline of the delivery towards the customer of the company that initially ordered this purchase item (author's experience).

Alongside this as a perhaps more apparent part of this phase, the financial background of possible suppliers is investigated, especially in the case of purchases worth several hundreds of thousands of euros or even more. This is to reduce the risk of the event in which the supplier company might go bankrupt in the middle of the delivery of the service or goods (Moody's, 2024). Besides this investigation, many major companies, including many automotive OEM's, original equipment manufacturers, are nowadays also requiring their suppliers to perform a full

TCO analysis (Fishman, 2024). And even though this requirement is meant primarily to reduce the financial risk of the company ordering the goods or services in the first place, it also greatly helps the suppliers to understand the cost elements related to the goods and/or services being requested for quotation, which reduces the financial risk of the supplier company (author's experience).

Once the quotations have been received and verified with supplier candidates that the scope of delivery, requested delivery time and other details have been understood correctly by the seller and buyer, and the supplier or suppliers have been selected, the rest of the work until the final phases of this delivery will be much easier than it would have been without proper initial specification documentation.

Besides the creation of the specification documentation and other work packages related to a technical purchase, it is also necessary to understand the cost elements of the initial purchase in terms of TCO. These elements vary greatly depending on what is being purchased, but for example, the typical list for purchasing some production line equipment includes the following in a thorough cost breakdown template, known as a CBD in the professional language:

➤ engineering, which can be informed as one price or, depending usually on the magnitude of delivery scope, shared for example between
  ○ tooling design
  ○ simulation
  ○ layout work
  ○ ergonomics design
➤ manufacturing, which can be shared for example between
  ○ hardware; mechanical and electrical/automation
  ○ manufacturing work
    ▪ even this can be shared in phases, such as cutting, machining etc.
➤ delivery including mention of INCOTERMS, to which we shall return later in this book
➤ installation and commissioning
➤ spare parts
➤ other work if included in the initially requested scope
➤ optional additional components, goods or services.

As mentioned before this list, this is only an example that highly depends on what is being ordered. And despite this phase of initial purchase in TCO can last a year or even longer, this is far from the only aspect of the TCO of a technical purchase. Once the equipment has been delivered, installed, commissioned and tested, we come to the next aspect, operation costs.

1.3.2 Operation

We could easily assume that once the equipment has been installed, commissioned and tested, it is ready to be put in use to run the production directly. And with a direct replacement investment with a piece of equipment very similar to its predecessor, this might very well be the case. However, the more things are changing in the entire production line around this one piece of equipment, the further from reality this assumption gets. But before we proceed onto this topic, I want to explain why I have chosen to differ from the cost elements allocated in this part compared to the categorisation introduced in the opening section of this Chapter 1.3. I've chosen to do this way because, based on my experience, installation and commissioning are often included in the initial purchase, the entire quotation of the equipment in question. But let's get back to the topic of operation costs.

Operation after installation, especially when the complete production process is either completely new, or a heavily modified version of an old one, has two aspects to it:

1. production process ramp-up and

2. line personnel qualification.

These both play their part on the "stage of TCO" because there are several variables related to both aspects. Production process ramp-up contains an immense quantity of cost elements that can vary greatly depending on multiple things. But to avoid repetition, let's focus on those cost elements that are at least partially unique to the ramp-up phase and stabilize once running what could be called regular production after ramp-up. Being a very complex topic, the testing, quality development and capacity ramp-up during this phase requires very careful planning on many aspects. Firstly, to successfully develop the process quality and test, validate and develop the process capacity, a lot of test parts are needed. And if the product that will be produced on the production line in question is still very new or especially if the product is still in the development phase, many of these test parts are still prototype parts. These prototype parts can cost even up to one hundred times the cost of their serial production equivalents or even more (Scholz, year unknown). This means the design maturity level of these parts must be considered carefully when trying to minimize the total cost of ownership within the key restrictions such as project schedule and required levels of quality and capacity of the production process at each phase of the ramp-up before the start of the production.

This brings us to the key goals of the ramp-up phase: product and process quality and process capacity targets during and after the ramp-up phase. These also have a multitude of TCO effects both directly in the amount of effort (=labour) required to reach these targets and the test parts consumed in the process and indirectly for example through changing or unclear quality specifications. Especially the latter is why also in the TCO point of view it is of utmost importance that the quality and capacity requirements have been set very clearly and specifically both for the time of the regular production and phases before it and that all these requirements have been aligned and agreed with the customer well before this phase starts. And not only with the customer; from the TCO and organisational point of view, it is equally important that all the internal stakeholders related to this ramp-up phase have understood these requirements similarly, too. If this is the case, it creates a stable and constructive foundation for pushing towards these goals as a team without unnecessary conflicts that might arise from multiple different understandings of these requirements, costing the entire project team both time and money.

Besides the process ramp-up, also the qualification of the production personnel, who will eventually take over the responsibility of running the line, must be taken care of to avoid unnecessary production stoppages and delays from human mistakes possibly caused by lack of qualification concerning the production process in question. Assuming that most of the production line personnel are already working in the company and have worked at the previous production lines, the key factor affecting the required scope of this qualification period is the amount of new technology to be operated compared to previous production lines. And this new technology does not only cover new technological advancements in the industry but also new ways to operate existing technology and, especially with automated solutions, if the technology has been provided by the suppliers previously unknown to the production personnel. For example, different manufacturers may use PLC or robot software that differs from each other, which sets additional qualification requirements to the production personnel.

Besides these topics, which may mostly be handled by the in-house personnel, in many cases external support might be needed for the ramp-up phase. And even though this is a temporary increase in expenses in personnel, this might even have an optimizing effect on the TCO of the whole production process due to the specialized knowledge by the external support personnel to tackle potential issues in the production ramp-up phase and any issues that otherwise could end up being the underlying root cause behind very costly production delays and stoppages (author's experience).

Last but not least, but on the contrary, we come to the operation costs beyond the ramp-up phase. And even though many of these expenses are also valid in the ramp-up phase, it usually only lasts a very short time compared to the product lifecycle in production, which means these expenses are much bigger in scale in the everyday running of the production process. These expenses include:

- ➢ wages of personnel to run the production process

- ➢ energy and water consumption of the production process and

- ➢ facilities in which the production process is being run, either owned or rented by the company

  - ○ also repairs of the facilities.

From total cost of ownership point of view, and in the means of expenses for the company, the wage costs of the personnel running the production process don't only include their salaries, but depending on the national or regional legislation, things like employer share of pension payments, compulsory insurance charges, work health arrangements, fringe subsidies and, for example, overtime. And depending on the working time laws, overtime alone can be even such a major cost element that it is well worthwhile to compare the TCO between having the bare minimum of personnel employed directly at the production line and having in addition springers, process operators and so on. What makes overtime a very expensive option is all the overtime extras for the workers secured through collective agreements between unions. For example, here in Finland, in the technological industry, a worker gets a 50% additional salary for the first two hours of overtime daily and a 100% additional salary after the first two hours. In addition, when the weekly overtime exceeds eight hours over the regular working time, every single overtime hour yields 100% wage on top of the regular salary even if on that exact day these hours would fall within the regular working hours. Besides that, there is another 100% additional wage for working on Sunday or a bank holiday, such as Ascension Day. Lastly, there's a fourth 100% extra wage if the weekly resting period of consecutive 35 hours is not fulfilled. This extra is paid for all the working hours that are worked during this resting period (Technology Industry Employers of Finland, 2024). All these additional overtime charges are well deserved, because the workers are sacrificing their time for resting, hobbies and time with family for the benefit of their employers but in practice the overtime, especially in bigger regular volumes, is so expensive, that it becomes very important to determine the amount of production personnel correctly already in the planning phase.

Indirectly operating expenses of the equipment include also accounting and legal fees, bank charges and office supplies (Kenton, 2024), but most of these are usually calculated either entirely or mostly into fixed costs because they're mostly required "anyway" to run the entire organisation besides the direct production process, so these are not included in the TCO comparison of the single pieces of equipment.

Next, we come to the process utilities, which include electricity, process heating, process cooling, waste treatment and air-pollution management (Chen et al., 2014). These are highly dependent on the types and volumes of machinery used in the production process and on the related technological solutions, for example, whether using a centralized or localized process cooling system.

Lastly, a big TCO element of the production process is the facilities in which the production is being run. Even in this context, when designing a new production line, there might be multiple scenarios to consider and multiple considerations to make; does the production line fit entirely in a possibly vacant area within currently existing facilities or in the place of a currently existing production line? If planned in the place of a currently existing production line, do the timing of the end of production for the current product and start of production for the new one allow the current production process being replaced with a new one? How different is the new production process from the existing one, meaning how extensive modifications it might require in utility connections or if the total input quantity of one or more process utilities into the entire facility needs to be altered?

Another scenario might be installing and commissioning the production process, for example, in a facility owned by the company; a facility that has recently or longer ago been in a different use but since then the company could not utilize this facility. In such a case, especially it's been long since the facility has been utilized for any similar kind of use as it's now being planned for, it is vital to ensure all the condition requirements in this facility are met to make sure it will be suitable for the intended use.

Performing all these clarifications already in the planning phase might sound time consuming and expensive, and might often require external, highly specialized expertise to give reliable answers to all these questions. But this can still be very cheap in relation to a potential alternative: project delays, panic solutions, unnecessary work health and safety risks, damage to the reputation of the company because of failing to do this necessary phase when it should have been done. Which is why they're also a crucial part of TCO when planning a production line. And speaking of TCO, next we come to the next, unfortunately often overlooked parts of the Total Cost of Ownership: maintenance and downtime.

1.3.3 Maintenance

The reason I consider this part of TCO often being overlooked is because I have seen or heard it multiple times: cost saving targets set by the top management and/or owners of the company leading to for example layoffs or freezing of recruitment processes within maintenance function of the company. After all, the regular responsibilities of maintenance workers include tasks like:

➢ inspecting buildings, systems and/or equipment regularly to identify any potential issues and troubleshooting these issues

➢ repairing faulty equipment or components or scheduling repairs if a specialist is required

➢ performing routine and preventive maintenance and

➢ maintaining a record of maintenance and repair tasks (ServiceChannel, 2024).

In addition to these tasks, e.g. regular inspections, lubrication and adjustments of the equipment are taken care of by the maintenance department (Graco Inc., 2024).

And now we get to why maintenance is an important part in the aim to reduce the total cost of ownership of a production process: If we don't maintain the equipment as it should be done, the savings targeted with the cost cutting in the maintenance department can lead to additional costs far exceeding these savings. "How is this possible?", we might ask. The "trouble" with skipping on the maintenance is that it increases the likelihood of much more expensive production stoppages and equipment failures. Let's illustrate this with a practical example including calculations.

Example 2: Because of reduced production volume needs the company lays off three maintenance workers out of the total quantity of 8 for seven months to reduce salary costs, taking a big risk with the current production process, knowing that a lot of scheduled maintenance had already previously fallen behind due to the lack of maintenance personnel to perform it on time.

The resulting reduction in salary costs is 3 persons x salary costs of 5 000 €/month (including pension and insurance costs etc.) x 7 months = 105 000 €. However, the risk is realized during this time multiple times, resulting in a multitude of line stoppages, 6 of which can be traced back to the lack of maintenance. These 6 stoppages last 6 hours each on average, resulting in wasted production time of 36 hours in total. Not wanting to fail to meet the monthly production volume targets and taking the risk of resulting worsening of the reputation of the company, the management decides to create a catch-up plan that consists of 4 Saturdays of overtime, 9 h each. Since the production stoppages affected the entire production, all employees on the production line, 40 workers, are needed to work on these 4 Saturdays of overtime. Using the previously described overtime renumeration system used in Technological Industry in Finland and an assumed monthly salary cost of 4 500 €/worker (= hourly average of 28,13 € when calculating with 160 h per month) on average, we can calculate that the execution of this catch-up plan ends up costing much more in total, all things considered.

- ➢ Wage costs per worker per Saturday = 28,13 €/h (average hourly salary cost) x 8 h x 1,5 (salary multiplier for the first 8 h of weekly overtime) + 28,13 €/h x 1 h x (salary multiplier for the weekly overtime hours beyond first 8 hours) = 393,82 €
    - ○ The work is done in such hours that it will not affect the weekly resting period, so no fees are paid for this
- ➢ This means that running the production on all four Saturdays of the month, 9 h each, means all this costs: 4 Saturdays x 40 people x 393,82 € per employee per Saturday in labour costs = 63 011,20 €.

Additionally, of the three maintenance workers that were laid off, two found a new employer and resigned shortly after, resulting in another 7 500 € of recruitment costs.

And just when the management could let a sigh of relief, having successfully implemented the catch-up plan, a highly complex piece of process equipment broke down. This breakdown could also be traced back to the lack of maintenance. Turned out the maintenance of this machine had been skipped for so long that nobody in the company had the competence to carry out the repairs. For this purpose, three specialists from the company that supplied the machine had to be booked for the repairs. Including one trip to first inspect the machine and order the required parts and the second one to repair and adjust the machine and train the company's personnel to operate and service the machine correctly the whole thing cost another 55 000 €. All this means the planned savings of 105 000 € in labour costs turned into 20 511,20 € of additional, unplanned expenses, which comes from the total expenditure of 125 511,20 € - the 105 000 € saved in labour costs by laying off the maintenance work.

Another way to reduce maintenance costs more sustainably is by:

- ➢ ensuring the availability of clear maintenance instructions and service schedules of the process equipment in all official communication languages in the company

> ➤ designing the process equipment with ease of maintenance in mind, meaning for example that all the servicing can be without very specialized tools or knowledge and that components are installed in such an order and location that replacing one component won't require a complete dismantling of the whole machinery.

The events and the related cost elements in the calculation example above are fictional, but this could very well happen in real life. The figures in the calculation are only for example but still realistic. But it could have ended much worse financially, resulting in downtime that cannot be made up for with a catch-up plan. And this brings us to the next topic.

1.3.4 Downtime

Many of the categorisations of TCO include downtime as a part of maintenance. However, maintenance downtime and shutdowns are a small cost compared to unplanned downtime that may result for example of lack of maintenance, which is why also the main categorisation used in this book turns this into its own part of TCO calculation (Graco Inc., 2024). Firstly, unplanned downtime in an industrial process is often caused either by an error in human action or error, or malfunction in machine operation or a disruption in the supply chain. And even though the primary reason leading to this issue might be even more obvious, it still takes a root cause analysis to understand the root cause that led to the issue that caused the downtime. This way, it is possible to implement preventive long-term measures proactively to prevent similar issues or malfunctions occurring in the same or different locations within the same company (SixSigma.us, 2024). And this root cause analysis takes time of process personnel, such as process engineers, supervisors and quality engineers. Secondly, the work of process operators is delayed, which means the work likely needs to be completed on overtime, costing more money than if it had been done in the regular working time as shown in the calculation example in the previous section. Thirdly, some production stoppages cannot be solved with the in-house knowledge available in the company but require specialist support instead, either from the company that initially supplied the faulty machinery or from an external company. This quickly available, on-call support can be highly expensive, and maintaining a service contract for such a service usually isn't free, either. Fourthly, all the lost production costs money to the company, both directly and indirectly. The most apparent direct cost is the amount of revenue the company would have made per product minus the variable costs that were "saved" because of not being able to run the production due to an unplanned stoppage. These "savings" in variable costs are insignificant because, for example, to save from labour costs, the company would need to plan the production downtime beforehand to adjust the workforce it calls in accordingly. Thus, we can calculate this third cost element directly as the amount of production lost times average € per product. Of course, this financial loss can be mitigated with a catch-up plan and executing such a plan successfully, but as demonstrated in the previous calculation example, this is not always so straightforward. But it can still very well be cheaper to try to catch up than not to try. And this is mostly due to potentially the biggest financial loss due to production stoppages: If production stoppages become such a huge issue that they start hindering the punctuality and quality of product delivery by the company, they pose a huge risk to the reputation of the company, hindering sales of both existing and especially new, upcoming products. So, in the worst case, a multitude of long-lasting production stoppages can even put a company out of business (Yadav, 2023).

1.3.5 Production

Next, we come to the production costs. In some of the TCO categorisations, these are included in the same category with operation costs. But these are more focused on the cost elements of running the machinery in the production. For example, different machinery for the same purpose might have a different output in quantity and quality and different effects on the environment (Graco Inc., 2024). This comparison is valid in many kinds of purchase decisions:

1. comparison between different purchase options for the same need
2. comparison between different technological solutions for the same dilemma
3. whether to invest to a new technological solution or maintaining the currently existing one.

In any of these comparisons, it is very relevant to consider distinct quality and quantity outputs of different technological solutions, because these affect the total cost of ownership of the production process. The quality and quantity outputs, benefit inputs one way or the other also affect the return on investment calculations related to this investment.

Besides these cost elements, wear parts and direct process materials fall into this category, such as weld electrode tips in spot welding or welding wire in the MIG brazing process. Another way to optimize the total cost of ownership is to utilize multipurpose machinery when possible. This can be done, for example, with an industrial robot that might be utilized for several distinct purposes, but careful attention must be paid to what different operations can be combined under one robot (author's experience).

1.3.6 Remaining value

The last category of total cost of ownership is the remaining value, which, when calculating the total cost of ownership, is deducted from the other cost elements. Remaining value refers to the estimated value of an asset at the end of its useful life (Tuovila, 2024). Basically, this remaining value can be positive, 0 € or negative. A positive value as an estimate means the company is expecting it will sell the asset onwards upon the end of its useful life in the production process. 0 € as the remaining value means the asset will be given away or utilised as reuse equipment, and a negative value practically means the asset will be disposed of, which causes further expenses for the company to pay. The difference between a positive and a negative value can be even dozens of thousands of euros, which is why it is important to plan and consider several distinct options what to do with the asset at the end of its useful life already well ahead of this point of time approaching.

Selling the equipment might not necessarily mean the asset is sold to another company or private individual who can use the equipment further. It can also mean the equipment is sold to a scrapping company as scrap. Sometimes this is the only option to make at least a bit of money with the equipment that is not useful to the company, but this should not be the default option because for example scrap metal is usually worth only one or two hundred euros per ton or even less, depending on the type of metal the equipment is made of and the market price for scrap metal (author's experience).

Now that we have covered the basic categories of Total Cost of Ownership, we're getting well equipped to gain an understanding of how to implement and apply TCO in a working organization, starting with the general topics and, later in the book, advancing further at this through different utilization aspects and business functions in which to apply TCO. Let's set sail towards the next island on this fascinating cruise on the waves of this interesting concept.

2 HOW TO IMPLEMENT AND APPLY TCO

Now that we have covered the very basics of Total Cost of Ownership, we get to the next part. Personally, I consider this as a part of the basics, because what would be the purpose of professional knowledge without applying it in practice and trying to implement it in the corporate culture? This requires a lot of brainwork, which is why this could be paired with the picture of The Thinker by the French sculptor Auguste Rodin, since it's widely considered as the symbol of human intellect. Unfortunately, I shall not be able to do so due to potential copyright issues.

In this chapter we cover topics such as the most common situations in which TCO can be applied, after which we cover the basics of value engineering and value analysis. The reason I have included these topics within this book is that they're highly useful in applying TCO on further topics way beyond purchasing and supply chain, especially in R&D, Simultaneous Engineering and organisational dilemmas. Aside from these aspects, TCO is, or at least should be, one of the key concepts for any cost engineer.

After this, we switch to practical applications of TCO:

- ➢ how to calculate TCO including examples
- ➢ related financial KPI's and how to calculate these KPIs
- ➢ management commitment and its importance to implementing TCO in a working organisation
- ➢ how to implement TCO in a working organisation and
- ➢ benefits, aspects and special considerations of TCO to end the whole part A of this book.

So once again, let's raise the anchor and set the sail towards how to apply TCO.

2.1 In what kinds of situations can TCO be applied?

Based on the research done in the making of this book, traditionally TCO has been applied mostly in purchasing, supply chain management and ICT. In a sense, this is understandable, since they both are vast topics that include a multitude of various cost elements, often forming a big proportion of the overall expenses in business. In purchasing, TCO can be applied, for example, when comparing different options of similar technical solutions for a dilemma in the production process, in which case the TCO comparison between different purchase options might be very straightforward.

However, this is often not the case when comparing very different technical solutions for the same dilemma in the production process due to potentially very different cost components of the purchase. This makes the collaboration with technical experts at both, the production process and of the proposed technical solutions vital to avoid missing major cost components in comparison. Of course, even before we get to compare different technical solutions in TCO, it is very important to prepare comprehensive TCO templates for the supplier candidates to fill in during the RFQ phase. But more about this in Section 12.2, Procurement & TCO.

Another purchasing-related aspect in which TCO is highly useful is make or buy decisions. These can be another complex subject, which requires extensive general knowledge both technically and commercially to understand the cost elements and related risks concerning both options, make or buy. And another slightly similar use of TCO is reshoring considerations, which focuses on bringing the manufacturing closer to the final assembly location (Cephas, 2022).

Aside from these, perhaps more traditional applications of TCO, it also has its uses in cost engineering, the product development process and simultaneous engineering. The reason these topics "deserve" to be covered in TCO is due to their immense cost-saving potential. The earlier a decision is made in the lifecycle of a product, the bigger the resulting losses or savings usually are due to each decision having a multitude of indirect effects on various aspects related to the lifecycle of the product (Collins & Hull, 2002). The cost impact of decision making during the product development phase can be up to 80% of the total life-cycle costs of the product (Advice-Manufacturing, 2024).

As mentioned in the opening section of this chapter, TCO goes very strongly hand in hand also with Value Engineering (VE) and Value Analysis (VA). In principle, these two concepts are very similar but applied in different phases of the product life cycle; applied in the product development process, value engineering focuses on the new products while value analysis concerns the existing products. These both involve teamwork and focus on reducing cost, improving function or both (Advice-Manufacturing, 2024). As these definitions show, when combining them with TCO, these concepts are highly useful in setting up the working organisation, developing an existing organisation or developing an existing production process or a product design.

And lastly, and perhaps the "furthest away" from the traditional uses of TCO, are the business stakeholders and, even if the furthest away from the most common uses of TCO, the most important aspect: people. And this aspect is the most important because it's us humans who run working organisations and work in them.

2.2   Value Engineering and Value Analysis

Value Engineering (VE) and Value Analysis (VA) go hand in hand with TCO. And the reason behind this is that an excellent understanding of the TCO of the product helps us understand the full picture of cost effects in decision making concerning both the product development phase and the existing product. But before diving deeper into this fascinating topic, let's try to understand what these two concepts mean in practice.

Value engineering is a process in which the target is to identify opportunities to reduce or even remove unnecessary costs while making sure that quality, performance, reliability and other critical factors will at least meet, or even exceed, the customers' expectations. And succeeding at this requires multidisciplinary teamwork between representatives of all the stakeholders. After all, the ultimate target is to reduce costs without sacrificing, for example, the quality or performance of the product (Dell'Isola, 1997). Value analysis, on the other hand, concerns existing products and their specifications and requirements (Reuter, 1968). Value Analysis is a relatively old method; its roots date back to the World War II, when reducing costs while maintaining the essential functionality was the primary focus in military projects (van der Schans et al., 2001). Value engineering also has its roots in the time of World War II, in the work done at General Electric by a procurement engineer called Larry Miles (Lane Davis, 2004).

Value engineering and value analysis are also valuable additions to tools and methods available to reduce the total cost of ownership (van der Schans et al., 2001). To understand the connection between these two methods and TCO, it is important to first define how value is measured. It is defined with the following function:

$value = \dfrac{functionality}{costs}$. And why the value engineering and value analysis go hand in hand with TCO is because in both methods both functionality and value must be defined in their broadest sense. And what would be a better method for defining the costs in their broadest sense than Total Cost of Ownership? Of course, value is not an objective definition, but depends on multiple factors, such as functionality, sensory impact, unconscious associations, conscious associations, access and convenience (EMyth, 2024). On top of that, functionality can also be defined in several ways, such as through:

- ➢ capacity
- ➢ product quality
- ➢ production flexibility

➢ fewer months to start of production (van der Schans et. al., 2001).

However, in the cost part of the value analysis and value engineering, understanding the Total Cost of Ownership of each optimization or improvement topic at hand is of great help in efforts of truly increasing the value. As in so many other applications of TCO, also in this its strongest point is the design to bring out all interdependent cost elements, which helps the whole multidisciplinary team to understand what kind of cost effects their decision making might have, in which phase of the product life cycle and how great these cost effects might be.

Even though value engineering and value analysis are mostly used in the development of new and existing products, the same principle, functionality over value, can also be applied to setting up a new or developing the structure of an existing organization and routine tasks in it. Each routine task has its own functionality that should be achieved at minimal to reasonable costs. In practice, this means that every single routine activity and function, for example, in a project must contain clear objectives and key performance indicators, KPIs, to measure the value of the task or function to the entire project. Through these KPI's the effectiveness of potential development measures can then be evaluated and improved even further. For example, a financial follow-up of the project contains certain tasks, such as cash flow and liquidity forecasts built on the information or forecast of the timing and sums of payments coming from customer(s) and the same of the payments going out to suppliers. The complexity of building up a liquidity forecast of course depends on the complexity of the project in question, but many other factors also affect the complexity, such as:

➢ how many overlapping reports are needed to create these forecasts

➢ how clear and easy the cash flow and liquidity forecasts are for the project personnel and management to understand

➢ how good the availability of the data is to build up these forecasts

➢ how reliable the available data is

➢ how well structured the data is and

➢ how well the responsibilities have been defined between the functions and teams within the project ➜ is there something that might be in the "grey" area, thus not included in the forecasts at all or having been entered in the forecasts multiple times but using different naming?

This example is only one of the many about the use of value analysis and value engineering in a project organisation, based on my experience working on projects. We shall discuss the topics of applying TCO in project and office work more in Chapter 4, but now we shall move on to the wider context of value engineering and value analysis, which is *cost engineering*.

2.3   Cost Engineering and TCO

Increasing competition in the market, risks and uncertainties pose many challenges to project management, one of which is avoiding cost overruns. Cost engineering techniques bring a lot of value in tackling this challenge. These techniques include things like cost estimation, cost control, cost forecasting, economic studies and risk management. However, while cost engineering alone may focus only on the project lifecycle (Macedo, 2024, p. 1), combined with Total Cost of Ownership it can cover the whole product lifecycle instead of "only" the project lifecycle (author's experience).

Cost engineering contains several basic concepts, many of which are common also to, for example, management accounting:

- cost vs. price
- labour
- material
- equipment
- direct and indirect costs
- overheads
- fixed, semi-fixed and variable costs
- cost breakdown structure and
- CAPEX and OPEX (Macedo, 2024, p. 1).

Understanding all these topics is crucial also to calculate the Total Cost of Ownership correctly. Aside from these concepts, cost engineering also contains, for example, quick cost estimation methods, such as cost per capacity or per physical dimension, factor method and parametric equation, as well as some more detailed methods (Macedo, 2024, pp. 32-52). All these methods benefit greatly from the understanding of TCO, because it is of great assistance in identifying the interdependencies between different cost elements in the cost estimation phase. This gives a more solid decision-making basis when moving on to a cost optimization phase, for example, of making quotations for potential customers, because with the help of TCO it is much easier to understand the big picture of costs. One simple example is the balance between automation rate and manual labour; making some process phase automated often increases investment costs but then saves money later in running costs of that same process. One example like this, and many more, are introduced in TCO calculation exercises in the next section 2.4.

Besides cost estimations and quotation calculations, TCO is of great importance also in cost forecasting during the project, and even more so when trying to mitigate the risk of overrunning the total budget. Especially when in a difficult overall financial situation, a company might face a huge pressure on cutting down on costs in a project that is forecasting a budget overrun. However, instead of single and separate cost-cutting measures, with the help of TCO we can be more certain to secure actual savings in costs instead of causing even a bigger increase in costs elsewhere within the same project when we cut costs in some other aspect. Of course, the TCO concept alone doesn't guarantee reaching actual cost savings without understanding the technical interdependencies of different aspects and functions (author's experience). This is why Cost Engineering Academy also states: "A good cost engineer is a technician at heart, but one who can dissect a project into stages" (Cost Engineering Academy, 2024). However, without TCO, the chances of turning the targeted cost savings into a further increase in costs elsewhere are much greater.

2.4 Practical applications of TCO

As described previously in the section 2.1, there are multiple ways to apply TCO some of which being a comparison of different purchase options for the same technological dilemma, a comparison between whether to stick to the currently existing technical solution or replacing it with something else and make/buy comparison. And these three cases shall also serve as our practical examples of how to calculate the total cost of ownership. Please note that all the figures used in these calculations are imaginative and must be investigated in the company to calculate the Total Cost of Ownership on a similar subject. But before we can start with the first example, we must define two perhaps quite theoretical, yet highly useful terms within this context: Mean Time to Repair (MTTR) and Mean Cost to Repair (MCTR). MTTR is defined as total time spent on repairs divided by the quantity of repairs (IBM, year unknown) and MCTR as total money spent on repairs divided by the quantity of repairs. However, the latter includes not only the parts themselves but also the production or quality loss while out of use, scrap created by the failure, labour and other potential costs to restore the device back to the same level as it was before the repair (Schneider Electric, 2015).

2.4.1 Comparison of different options for the same technological dilemma

In this first calculation example, we shall compare three different suppliers for spot weld guns for an automated process, to be operated with robots. For the sake of simplicity, we shall assume all the guns to be of a similar type and the production process to be repeating similar configuration on this front, meaning one weld timer is required per two weld guns. In this case this means 186 weld guns and 93 weld timers.

The operating speed of weld guns is also assumed to be the same regardless of the manufacturer, meaning we shall need the same amount of weld guns, whichever supplier we end up choosing. The production process, in which we are planning to use these weld guns, runs in three shifts, five days a week, each shift having an effective working time of 7,3 hours out of 8 hours of the total shift duration, 230 working days per year. The product lifecycle in production is 7 years, and the required number of weld spots per product is 4 000 pieces, with the average volume of 40 000 products per year. While engineering the production process concept, the manufacturing engineering team also got a confirmation from the facility unit, that there is plenty of capacity available for electricity and all the other required process utilities, which means we won't need to consider these in this calculation example. However, finding these out is necessary whenever designing a new production process either to a new facility or a replacement process in the place of an existing one with any increase in any of the utility requirements.

These technical requirements of the weld guns, along with other technical specifications, such as process descriptions and quality specifications, were sent to three supplier candidates, along with the information that the equipment is needed on site and installed on site in 21 weeks from sending the purchase order. The supplier candidates responded with quotations containing the following figures:

Table 1. Weld gun and timer quotations.

Supplier	Supplier A	Supplier B	Supplier C
Weld gun price	14 000 € / pce	10 000 € / pce	11 000 €/pce
Welding timer price	16 100 € / pce	14 200 € / pce	15 000 €/pce
Energy consumption, weld gun	0,36 kWh	0,40 kWh	0,30 kWh
Energy consumption, weld timer	0,48 kWh	0,44 kWh	0,46 kWh
Electricity price	0,09 €/kWh	0,09 €/kWh	0,09 €/kWh
Other required process utilities	None	None	None
Delivery time + INCOTERMS	12-16 weeks FCA	24 weeks DAP	16-20 weeks DDP
Extra charge for catch up	10 % of the total value per -1 week in delivery time	5 % of the total value per -1 week in delivery time	10 % of the total value per -1 week in delivery time
Delivery included in pricing	Yes, one delivery to deliver all equipment	Yes, one delivery to deliver all equipment	Yes, one delivery to deliver all equipment
Price of extra deliveries	3 000 € / delivery	5 000 € / delivery	2 000 € / delivery
Operating life with the required working time model	10 years	7 years	8 years
Duty charges (%)	None (from EU)	2,7 %	None (delivery duty paid)

Let's calculate the subtotals and total pricing of quotations in the two tables below for the sake of clarity.

Item / Supplier	Supplier A	Supplier B	Supplier C
Hardware pricing	186 x 14 000 € + 93 x 16 100 € = 4 101 300 €	186 x 10 000 € + 93 x 14 200 € = 3 180 600 €	186 x 11 000 € + 93 x 15 000 € = 3 441 000 €
Delivery charge for the first delivery	0 €	0 €	0 €
Schedule catch-up charge	Not required	5 % / week x 3 weeks x 3 180 600 € = 477 090 €	Not required
Duty charges	None (EU)	2,7 % x Hardware pricing = 85 876,2 €	None (Delivery Duty Paid)
VAT	None (EU)	12,0 % x Hardware pricing = 381 672 €	12,0 % x Hardware pricing = 412 920 €
Installation and commissioning fee	0 €	93 sets x 16 h/set x 90 €/h = 133 920 €	93 sets x 20 h/set x 75 €/h = 139 500 €
Total hardware pricing	**4 101 300 €**	**4 125 238,2 €**	**3 993 420 €**
Pricing considering savings in tip dressers		4 125 238,20 € - 150 000 € = 3 975 238,20 €	

Table 2. Weld gun and timer equipment pricing.

Supplier	Supplier A	Supplier B	Supplier C
Number of working hours during product lifecycle	7,3 h / shift x 3 shifts/day x 230 days/year x 7 years = 35 259 h	7,3 h / shift x 3 shifts/day x 230 days/year x 7 years = 35 259 h	7,3 h / shift x 3 shifts/day x 230 days/year x 7 years = 35 259 h
Total electricity consumption per h	2 x 0,36 + 0,48 kWh = 1,20 kWh	2 x 0,40 + 0,44 kWh = 1,24 kWh	2 x 0,30 + 0,46 kWh = 1,06 kWh
Total electricity	35 259 h x 1,20	35 259 h x 1,24	35 259 h x 1,06

costs	kWh x 0,09 €/kWh = 3 807,97 €	kWh x 0,09 €/kWh = 3 934,90 €	kWh x 0,09 €/kWh = 3 363,71 €
Total amount of work cycles for the equipment	186 x 40 000 x 7 = 52 080 000 pcs	186 x 40 000 x 7 = 52 080 000 pcs	186 x 40 000 x 7 = 52 080 000 pcs
Total amount of electrode tips required	52 080 000 pcs / 150 cycles / pce x 2 pcs / device = 694 400 pcs	52 080 000 pcs / 250 cycles / pce x 2 pcs / device = 416 640 pcs	52 080 000 pcs / 150 cycles / pce x 2 pcs / device = 694 400 pcs
Money spent on electrode tips	694 400 pcs x 500 € / 10 000 pcs = 34 720 €	416 640 pcs x 370 € / 10 000 pcs = 15 415,68 €	694 400 pcs x 500 € / 10 000 pcs = 34 720 €
Mean Time to Repair	15 min	15 min	15 min
Mean Cost to repair	1 000 €	1 500 €	1 250 €
Total maintenance cost (4 service, items 4 times a year each)	7 years x 1 000 € x 4 items x 4 service item = 112 000 €	7 years x 1 500 € x 4 items x 4 service item = 168 000 €	7 years x 1 250 € x 4 items x 4 service item = 140 000 €
Total money spent on operation	3 807,97 € + 34 720 € + 112 000 € = 150 527,97 €	3 934,90 € + 15 415,68 € + 168 000 € = 187 350,58 €	3 363,71 € + 34 720 € + 140 000 € =178 083,71 €
Total lifecycle cost	4 251 827,97 €	**4 162 588,78 €**	4 171 503,71 €

The calculation shows that supplier B is the cheapest. However, if the manufacturing engineering team decides to pre-pone the delivery by one more week to mitigate the risk of delay at the start of process runs, the price is increased by another 5% of the purchase price, making the total price 4 162 588,78 € + 5% x 3 180 600 € = 4 321 618,78 €.

This reflects real life in business, savings versus risk.

What other cost-saving potential can you think of in this equation? Use your own experience and/or online sources to find answers.

2.4.2 Process development

A process engineer has proposed that one process phase should be automated to improve safety, quality and ergonomics. To back this up, together with work health services, the process engineer has estimated the process automatization leading to a decrease of 3 mild and 1 severe injury per year. Furthermore, the process quality engineer has estimated that the automatization of this process phase would lead to total savings of 20 000 € per year in scrap.

Currently, the process involves manual gluing operations, employing three full-time employees with monthly wage costs of 3 000 €. The process has been operational for 1,5 years out of its 7-year lifecycle and the process engineer has determined together with the manufacturing engineering tea, that the lead time of the whole process modification including all the equipment, installation, commissioning and required quality assurance phases is 1 year. This leaves another 4,5 years of operating life for the new process. There's no reuse in sight for the process yet, so the plant director has instructed to do the payback period calculation based on the 4,5 years of operating life. As a side note from the author, payback period and other financial KPIs shall be deep-dived in the section 2.5.

The investment costs of the new process total at 370 000 € + additional operating expenses during the trial runs in the forms of test parts, total of 12 000 €. Additionally, the new process would consume the same amount of glue as the current process, but the electricity consumption would increase by 4,5 kWh from the current level of 2,5 kWh, bringing the total to 7,0 kWh. Currently the electricity price is 0,09 €/kWh and the long-term forecast shows a similar level for the next year. No further information is available, so the plant director has instructed to use this value at electricity pricing calculations. With the automated process, maintenance costs are expected to increase by 1 500 € per year from the current level of 1 000 €/year, but the maintenance manager has estimated that no additional maintenance personnel is needed due to this process change.

Let's calculate whether automatization has a payback period and if we can affect this in any way.

Process mode	Automated	Manual
Wage expenses over 4,5 years	None	3 operators x 4,5 years x 12 months/year x 3 000 € / month = 486 000 €
Scrap costs (reference level 30 000 €/year)	(30 000 - 20 000 €/year) x 4,5 years = 45 000 €	30 000 € / year x 4,5 years = 135 000 €
Investment costs	370 000 €	0 €
Test parts	12 000 €	0 €
Electricity consumption (230 days/year, 1 shift; 8 h/shift working time)	230 days/year x 8 h/shift x 7 kWh x 4,5 years x 0,09 €/kWh = 5 216,40 €	230 days/year x 8 h/shift x 2,5 kWh x 4,5 years x 0,09 €/kWh = 1 863,00 €
Maintenance costs	2 500 €/year x 4,5 years = 11 250 €	1 000 €/year x 4,5 years = 4 500 €
Total lifecycle costs	**443 466,4 €**	**627 363,4 €**
Payback period (total change costs divided by annual expenses of current process)	**= 443 466,40 € / (627 363,40 €/4,5 years) = 3,18 years = <u>3 years 2 months</u>.**	
Management decision	**Change approved**	

Since the payback period is more than 2 years, which is a "rule of thumb" guideline in some companies, how do you justify this process change to top management?

2.4.3 Make or buy

As for the third example, we move to another common investment decision: make or buy. In practice, this means deciding whether to manufacture a product in-house or purchasing it from an external supplier (Kenton, 2024), This is the traditional use of make or buy but with some adaptation, it can be also applied to services and e.g. project work. However, in this example, we shall focus on the product manufacturing.

In this example, the question is whether to manufacture an assembly in-house or to outsource it. The background data for the comparison is as follows:

> ➤ Production volumes are on average 45 000 pcs/year for 3 years.

- ➢ In-house production runs in one shift, five days a week.
- ➢ The assembly manufacturing includes spot welding and adhesive bonding.
- ➢ One assembly is required per product.
- ➢ The assembly manufacturer is responsible for the quality of the finished product towards its customer, who is responsible for the quality of the complete product towards its customer.
    - o This work remains unaffected, whether the assembly in question is outsourced or not
- ➢ This is only one of the many assemblies considered being outsourced.
    - o The outsourcing team is required in the project in any case, and the creation of technical specifications and getting the quotations for the assemblies is a part of the clarification required for the make or buy decision, anyway. This means that this part of the work shall not be considered applicable to the make or buy evaluation scope.
    - o However, the manufacturing of this assembly has some synergies with some of the other assemblies, which shows in relatively low investment needs by the supplier if manufacturing this assembly. Yet, the company considering the outsourcing cannot utilize these same synergies due to a much less flexible manufacturing process that has to be optimized around the whole product, not only between several single assemblies.
- ➢ In-house manufacturing of this assembly would not require additional workers in the production. This process is completely automated and does not add to the workload of internal logistics considerably.
- ➢ Delivering the required parts requires one full lorry per two weeks, and the freight costs are 350 € per full lorry.
- ➢ Production runs 46 weeks a year.
- ➢ Internal logistics costs of either delivering the complete assemblies from a warehouse or parts for the assemblies to the line are estimated to be the same.

The cost and pricing comparison between in-house manufacturing and is written down in the following table.

Make / Buy	Make	Buy
Investment costs	160 000 €	45 000 €
Assembly fee	-	2,6 €/pce
Process electricity costs for the buyer	5 kWh x 8 h x 230 days/year x 3 years x 0,09 €/kWh = 2 484 €	-
Freight costs	-	350 €/lorry x 23 lorries/year x 3 years = 24 150 €
Maintenance costs increase	1 000 €/year	-
Cost effect on the outsourcing of other assemblies if this one is made in-house	1,60 €/product => 1,6 € x 45 000 pcs/year x 3 years	
Total lifetime cost	**381 484 €**	**420 150 €**
Management decision	**Make**	

Table 3. Make or buy calculation 1.

To conduct a sensitivity analysis for this investment, the outsourcing team and supplier have defined that if the production volume is increased by 20% to 54 000 pcs/year, the supplier investments are increased by 15 000 € and in-house investments by 40 000 €. At the same time, 20% more freights are required between the supplier and the company. On the other hand, if the volume is increased, the supplier can sell the manufacturing of the assembly for 2,45 €/pce. Also, the cost effect on the outsourcing of other assemblies if this one is made in-house drops to 1,52 €/product. Electricity costs are also increased by 20%, maintenance costs remain unaffected.

Make / Buy	Make	Buy
Investment costs	200 000 €	60 000 €
Assembly fee	-	2,45 €/pce
Process electricity costs for the buyer	6 kWh x 8 h x 230 days/year x 3 years x 0,09 €/kWh = 2 980,80 €	-
Freight costs	-	350 €/lorry x 28 lorries/year x 3 years = 29 400 €
Maintenance costs increase	1 000 €/year	-
Cost effect on the outsourcing of other assemblies if this one is made in-house	1,52 €/product => 1,52 € x 54 000 pcs/year x 3 years	
Total lifetime cost	**452 220,80 €**	**486 300,00 €**
Management decision	**Make**	

For further consideration, you can ponder what measures the supplier could take to achieve more competitive pricing. For this exercise, let's assume the supplier profit margin is at the industry average, it needs all its employees to achieve the required production volumes, and it cannot affect the freight cost further since it has a binding contract with the freight company, selected on based on a tender process.

2.5   Related financial KPIs and calculations

There are several financial KPIs, Key Performance Indicators, to define the financial performance of a company. These are used to measure the financial performance of a company. Understanding these indicators is very important in many aspects of TCO work in the company, because by understanding the financial KPIs, TCO work can be:

➢ more easily "sold" to the management as a new idea when not yet in use in the company

- prioritized based on the financial targets of the company and the related strategic choices
- made more efficient when understanding what TCO elements affect which financial KPI (author's experience).

That said, the ultimate target of the TCO must be improving the long-term financial result of the company instead of "optimizing" between financial KPIs.

The first financial performance indicators of a company are revenue and change of revenue in percentage compared to the previous accounting period, such as a year. Revenue is defined as the total sales made from the business of the company from which subsidies, VAT and other direct taxes based on the total sales (Tilastokeskus, 2024). Revenue alone is a questionable financial performance indicator without comparing it to the revenue of other companies in the same business and to the revenue made by the same company in past years. Even though revenue is not directly affected by TCO work, it has two main relations to TCO:

1) Active and comprehensive TCO work greatly improves also the chances of additional sales by creating more possibilities to lower the pricing of the product without sacrificing functionality or vice versa, improving functionality without the need to increase the price. In other words, TCO brings a great deal of added value in this aspect.

2) Additional revenue gives a chance to bring in more funds to invest in software, equipment and so on to further improve TCO work in the company.

The second common financial performance indicator is gross margin, often expressed as a percentage of the total revenue. As a percentage of the total revenue, this is calculated using the following formula: $\frac{Revenue - Variable\ costs}{Revenue} \times 100\ \%$. In the TCO context, this is affected by successful TCO work through reduction of variable costs but also by the improved chances of increasing revenue, as described previously.

The third common financial performance indicator is EBIT, Earnings Before Interests and Taxes, also known as operating profit. In euros, this is calculated by deducting fixed costs, depreciation and amortization from gross profit. The resulting sum is then divided by the total revenue to reach the EBIT %. Besides the aforementioned benefits from TCO, EBIT can be improved with successful TCO work by having a positive effect on fixed costs in multiple ways, such as reducing the costs of management, marketing and warehousing.

The fourth common financial performance indicator is the net profit for the operating period, commonly a financial year (Järvenpää et al., 2013). This is commonly calculated as a percentage of the total revenue and is calculated by deducting interest income and interest expenses, any other costs besides variable and fixed costs and taxes from EBIT. Besides the above-described benefits of TCO on financial performance indicators until EBIT, this specific indicator gains positive effects from TCO through the high potential of lowering the interest costs by reducing the total need for a loan through improved revenue and reduced total costs, which in practice means that in a way TCO has double benefits on net profit.

Since TCO has a great potential of improving the overall financial result from year to year, it also has a great potential to benefit other financial performance indicators, such as return on capital employed (ROCE), return on assets (ROA) and quick ratio.

2.6   Management commitment

Top management commitment is one factor that can enhance the competitive advantage of a company. After all, top management is in a crucial position to determine the success of a company among its competitors (Jiwa et al., 2020). The importance of management commitment is also recognised in one of the main standards in the manufacturing industry, ISO 9001 Quality Management Systems. Roughly 15% of the text in this standard is dedicated to the responsibilities of management, because the system doesn't really work without top management commitment. The standard states, for example, the following: "5.1 Management Commitment.

Top management shall provide evidence of its commitment to the development and implementation of the quality management system and continually improving its effectiveness by:

a) communicating to the organization the importance of meeting customer as well as statutory and regulatory requirements,

b) establishing the quality policy,

c) ensuring that quality objectives are established,

d) conducting management reviews, and

e) ensuring the availability of resources."

Similar content is written in different words also, for example in ISO standard 14001 for Environmental Management System Requirements and OHSAS 18001 for OHS Management Systems, which further emphasizes the importance of management commitment. Additionally, if the senior management shows it doesn't commit to what is required of the organisation, the employees will also very easily feel that why should they, then, either (GrowEQ, 2023).

Then what does the management commit to when a company undergoes a change in the ways of working to make it possible to fulfil the requirements of successful TCO work? Based on my working experience in an engineering organisation and knowledge in leadership and organisational sciences, it isn't setting the cost-saving targets to be achieved with TCO but facilitating the change required in the ways of working to achieve what is aimed for with TCO. In practice, this contains several aspects, most of which lie within the contexts of organisation and functions within it and the mutual collaboration between and within functions. After all, one of the most certain ways to make sure the TCO implementation fails is to foster a siloed culture. This is such a major barrier to successful implementation of Total Cost of Ownership that it will be discussed more in detail in section 8.10.

Additionally, it is highly important to ensure that the financial basis of management rewarding is determined by the overall financial result of the company, not in the budget versus actuals of own cost centres of these managers. The reason behind this is that the former mostly encourages working together to achieve common goals. And even though the very common rationale behind the latter is "when all managers make their cost centres profitable, the overall profitability is improved", more often than not this will not work. And the root cause behind this is very much similar to why the cost-cutting method, that could be called a "cheese slicer", as it is called in Finnish, often fails. Because when actual costs are only optimized between cost centres without taking care of the big picture, there's a high risk that the cost-saving measures will only lead to even further increased costs elsewhere within the company, total cost effect increasing instead of decreasing. And this is especially important to acknowledge at the managerial level, because even though we are all grown-ups, the example shown by managers tends to be followed by their subordinates. And for this reason, the example that top management shows to middle management, and so on further down in the organisational hierarchy, is equally important.

All in all, the biggest critical factors of either success or failure of a change in the ways of working in an organisation are the people managing the organisation and working in it. Which is one reason why the topic Human aspect & TCO has been given its own part as Chapter 8.

2.7 How to implement TCO in a working organization

Understanding the basics of Total Cost of Ownership is crucial to be able to correctly and successfully transfer the theory into practice. Which is why it wouldn't make any sense to start this book with this part, either. TCO, just like any comprehensive change in some aspect of the ways of working, is a transformational change, and keeping this in mind is vital when implementing it into everyday life in a working organisation. Especially since all transformational changes face change resistance to some extent. If no measures are taken to help the people in the organisation adapt to the change, some might even end up leaving the company because of the change. And even if not leaving the company, resisting a change can be emotionally exhausting for the employees. But not all change resistance is negative, because it also opens chances for open discussion and debate (Robbins & Judge, 2022, p. 323), which can reveal crucial flaws in the approach towards TCO itself in the specific case of implementation or in the approach towards the transformational change. Both are excellent chances to learn new things and improve the process.

And besides, there are multiple ways to overcome change resistance, such as:

- ➢ communication
- ➢ having employees participate in the execution of the change
- ➢ building support and commitment
- ➢ developing positive relationships between organisational hierarchy levels and
- ➢ implementing changes fairly.

There are also some models for implementing a change successfully. Probably the best-known one is Kotter's Eight-Step Plan for Implementing Change. As its name tells, this model has eight phases:

1. Creating a sense of urgency by bringing up an intriguing reason the change is needed.
2. Form a group powerful enough to lead the change.
3. Create a new vision to guide the change and strategies to succeed in reaching this vision.
4. Communicate the vision throughout the organisation.
5. Help others act by reducing obstacles to the change and encourage risk taking and creative problem solving.
6. Plan, create and reward short-term "wins" that bring the organisation closer to the new vision.

7. Combine improvements, re-evaluate changes and make the needed adjustments in the new programs.

8. Strengthen the changes by demonstrating the relationship between new behaviours and organisational success. (Robbins & Judge, 2022, pp. 324-328).

Besides overcoming the change resistance, there is the matter of practical implementation of TCO in the working organisation. As described above, just like any major change, this requires a vision and strategies to achieve it. A lot of systematic work is required to get the change going. This can be done in many ways, but personally, I would recommend considering a few things when considering which way to approach the matter:

➢ What is the status of different areas of TCO in the company when starting the work?

➢ How to prioritize the work? If the more immediate aspects in time can be defined and if it is feasible to implement TCO in these aspects, this can be a good starting point, especially if relatively big cost savings can be achieved. Another prioritization criterion can be the estimated cost-saving potential.

➢ Since TCO implementation planning and execution often requires a lot of work, one person doing it all alone is not enough. Thus, a core team is required. If possible, this team should contain some people with relevant experience on TCO and some who don't but are experts in relevant fields of work. The former can take the lead of the implementation work while the latter bring in highly valuable viewpoints concerning both what they think needs to be developed and being the first ones whose reactions towards this change to observe. That said, these core team members, unless selected in a very authoritarian way by their corresponding managers, are often curious and positive about TCO to begin with, which means they typically show very little to no change resistance at all.

Whichever the criteria are selected, it is crucial to understand the big picture before starting the planning and implementation work. There are several reasons for this. The first one is that focusing on the big picture first enables:

➢ making sure the big picture of the TCO implementation is in line with the even bigger picture in the company: its vision and strategy to achieve that vision

➢ empowering the TCO team members by helping them see how the related work is tied to this bigger picture of the company

- ➢ illustrating the short-term wins described by Kotter as described previously in this section by building the illustration of the big picture in a manner that allows the follow-up of the progress
- ➢ reducing early change resistance by showing the organisation why the TCO development is being done, what can be achieved with it and how it is tied to the work of each member of the organisation.

Secondly, once the big picture of TCO development in a company has been formed, it is much easier to do task allocation and prioritization, making the work much more efficient. Additionally, based on my experience, it is very useful to construct the illustration of the big picture in such a manner that relevant new ideas for development aspects in the overall TCO development work can be introduced on the go, in which case this illustration also works as a checklist.

Aside from the formation of the big picture, planning and implementing the TCO in a working organisation, it also needs to be followed up to make it a standard approach. KPIs can and must be set for each element of TCO, starting with acquisition cost and ending with disposal costs. For example, the costs of maintenance and support can be reduced by investing in preventive maintenance and training of in-house personnel (Ignition, 2024). After all, preventive maintenance is almost always considerably cheaper than reactive maintenance, which is fixing and repairing after a system breakdown. These KPIs are then measured, tracked, monitored and reported against baseline and set targets and goals. Remaining competitive also requires constant improvement (Ignition, 2024).

And lastly, training is required to help the organisation understand what TCO is all about, why it is highly beneficial and how it can be utilised in different fields of work within the organisation. Based on my experience and the feedback I have received from the trainings I have arranged so far, I highly recommend training methods that involve engaging teamwork between people from different functions. After all, this is what is required also in real life to succeed at improving the overall profitability by finding real cost savings.

2.8   Benefits, considerations and aspects of TCO

As described in the previous section, understanding the benefits, potential restrictions and aspects of TCO is a superb "selling point" to help the senior management understand why implementing and utilizing TCO in the whole organisation is beneficial in so many ways.

However, one TCO model that could be applied in all fields of industry does not exist (Gartner, 2018). Aside from the most common uses of TCO already described, for example in section 2.4, it can be utilized in so many more ways beyond the "traditional" contexts of purchasing and supply chain management.

Let's take an imaginary example that could happen in real life: In a project, there is a phase during which the first products are built up throughout the entire production process and, once completed, they are inspected for any defects. The findings are then presented and discussed within a working group of representatives from various production departments to determine the most probable responsible departments for each defect. This phase of the project contains regular meetings within this working group to follow up on the actions taken to remove or reduce the impact of these defects. The representatives of different departments in these meetings are the ones responsible for coordinating this work within their corresponding production departments, but different people running their responsibility areas within these production departments are doing the technical improvements to tackle these defects. Basically, it would be possible to invite all these people to report the progress at the meeting. However, this would lead to a situation in which there are easily 20 people in the same 2-hour meeting going through the defects instead of 5 people otherwise actually required, given that there are three production departments and each of them has a representative who knows the ongoing actions just as well as the people doing the improvements in the production line.

Let's say the average hourly wage per person is 60 €. This means an unnecessary wage expense of 1 800 € per meeting. Given this meeting is a recurring one, occurring once a week during this phase, the total amount of money wasted during, for example, 10 weeks, is 18 000 € in this meeting arrangement alone. When putting this in context, this completely unnecessary spend is over 5 times the cost compared to the electricity expenses of one piece of process equipment for 7 years! As we shall discuss much more in depth, for example, in Chapter 4, understanding the monetary cost of different office work processes is crucial to being able to apply principles of TCO to topics beyond purchasing and supply chain management.

Besides this, TCO can be utilized for topics such as quality improvement and strategy work. Not only is TCO an excellent tool for economic scenario work in strategy work, but the superb potential it has to improve the financial situation of the company also creates an excellent foundation to do the investments needed to achieve the strategic goals of the company. TCO also contains mathematical programming models that help reduce subjectivity in supplier selection. Additionally, TCO can be utilized to conduct sensitivity analyses concerning cost management (Katholieke Universiteit Leuven).

Aside from these benefits, TCO is also highly applicable in the new product development process and simultaneous engineering when making an overall cost analysis of different options of technical solutions at product design and manufacturing. Speaking of manufacturing, TCO combined with value analysis, work study and Kaizen makes it also an excellent tool for the development of an existing production process. In addition, TCO principles can be applied in any typical function in a working organisation. And even though this "one way or another" may sound far-fetched, the working processes in the office, as described earlier in this section, can be optimized. And this is applicable to any function without compromising any activities in other functions as long as for example minimising the quantity of meeting participants doesn't become the only criteria in meeting invitations on the expense of successful stakeholder management, which also is one aspect of TCO. Stakeholder management in the context of TCO will be discussed further in Chapter 7.

However, even though there's a huge number of positives to successful implementation of TCO, it also requires a foundation to build on. Even though TCO principles can be applied to some extent based on almost any starting point, the biggest benefit can be yielded when there is the data available to do the required calculations to support decision making. Of course, this data is not always readily available when starting the work. In many cases, one of the first tasks is arranging the cost databases to support these calculations. There are several options for ICT software on the market to ease up this work and, even though some of them are quite pricey, their return on investment is still very good when compared to the other main option, gathering and storing the data to these databases manually. Even in many moderate-sized organisations, there might be only one to very few people doing this work, which means establishing these databases will easily take several months and even longer when this work is not the major share of the workload of these people. Aside from ICT software dedicated to cost engineering and other highly useful tools for TCO work, also Enterprise Resource Planning, ERP, software is highly beneficial for this, because much of the past price data can be found within the purchasing module of such software. ERP software is also highly useful for many other purposes. When understanding the capabilities of such software well and combining this knowledge together with the understanding of Total Cost of Ownership, "selling" the idea of having an ERP system in the company should not be too difficult if there are funds available for this. In addition, the application of TCO can be challenging, and the mathematical models included in TCO can be difficult to operate for the management. This complexity can also be disruptive, costly and time-consuming.

Besides the great help of ICT solutions, there are also organisational requirements for the successful implementation and upkeep of TCO optimization. One of the key competencies is understanding the technical interconnections behind the cost figures. This means, for example, understanding all the different cost elements related to a technical solution and how these cost elements might vary in price and form when selecting another technical solution for the same purpose. There are also several other organisational and human aspects of TCO, many of which shall be discussed further in Chapters 4 and 8. But here are some considerations that I would consider keys to successful TCO work:

➢ a personnel rewarding and incentive system that emphasizes the success of the collective instead of the success of the individual with topics of budget under-runs and overruns or other financial aspects

➢ promoting healthy cross-functional collaboration and other measures to minimize organisational silos

➢ willingness to plan long-term instead of short-term

➢ helping the whole team to find common motivations and work together, keeping in mind that it is the finished and sold a product that brings in the funds to pay all members of the organisation instead of focusing on single responsibilities as somehow separated assignments.

And these topics bring us to what I consider the main aspects of Total Cost of Ownership:

1. Monetary Aspect
2. Working Process Aspect
3. Quality Aspect
4. Strategy Aspect
5. Stakeholder Aspect
6. Human Aspect

These aspects shall be discussed further in the *part B* of this book, consisting of chapters 3 to 8. Understanding these aspects will also help us at deep-diving the topics of the *part C*. Onwards to the somewhat uncharted territories of "more" in the name of this book. Maybe we'll find some useful nautical charts on the way.

PART B – ASPECTS OF TCO

After the basics of Total Cost of Ownership, we shift our focus to what I call the *aspects of TCO*. These consist of:

- ➢ Monetary Aspect
- ➢ Working Process Aspect
- ➢ Quality Aspect
- ➢ Strategy Aspect
- ➢ Stakeholder Aspect
- ➢ Human Aspect

The monetary aspect is the most recognized in TCO literature. In practice, the monetary aspect contains finance and purchasing, which are some of the basic contexts of TCO. However, TCO is highly useful in several other aspects, too. The working process aspect contains topics such as meetings, importance of planning and resourcing, as well as waste in working processes and specifically in, for example, meetings and reporting.

Quality Aspect shifts our focus to how important quality is for overall TCO optimization. For instance, ramping up the production volume in a freshly built production line while focusing only on production volumes and neglecting quality can lead to very high scrap costs reaching even to millions of euros of wasted funds.

After this, we discuss the relationship of strategy and internal and external stakeholders and TCO. After all, successful stakeholder management can "work wonders" in overall TCO optimization by enabling enhanced decision-making and reducing the amount of working time wasted in having to fix the mistakes that might result from failures at stakeholder management. Also, the effects of successful TCO optimization on external stakeholders are discussed.

And last but not least for this chapter, we shift our focus to the human aspect of TCO. After all, it is us humans who run the organisations and work in them. Every human action has a consequence, and these consequences can either advance or hinder the overall financial result. We humans are complex creatures, and we can have an enormous impact on the total financial result of the company even without realizing it, for example, through spending our working time efficiently, working well together and solving problems together. On the other hand, worsening organisational commitment, for example, because of continuous layoffs and organisational silos, can hinder achieving what is ultimately pursued with TCO work – improving the overall financial result of the company. And personally, I prefer to add: Improving the overall financial result of the company sustainably, which to me means the result is improved by developing and using more efficiently what we already have, making investments with good payback periods and using the funds smartly and avoiding the waste. I strongly believe that this way companies can save much more money than with any kind of layoffs. This is one of my intrinsic motivations for writing this book in the first place: to try to open up opportunities to save money without having to lay off or fire people, affecting their income and feeling of purpose negatively.

Without further ado, let's set our sails to the fascinating archipelago that I call Aspects of TCO.

3 MONETARY ASPECT

As the abbreviation TCO stands for Total Cost of Ownership, we could easily be fooled into thinking that it is applicable only for visible costs, such as purchases and supply chain management contracts. However, as explained in the previous chapters, the whole point of TCO is to expand our view about costs in business operations beyond visible costs, as presented in the opening picture of part A. However, it is still very important to also discuss this perhaps the most obvious aspect of the concept. And the top motivation for this, at least to me, is that when we understand the monetary aspect of TCO broadly and can explain its benefits well, it is much easier to justify spending working hours and perhaps some investments in TCO planning, implementation and making it a part of working procedures in a company. Even during an economic downturn. The other rationale behind making this the first aspect of TCO is the whole main point, optimizing the total costs instead of partial optimization between different cost elements.

3.1 Cost structure and TCO

Cost structure is defined as the aggregate of fixed and variable costs that form the total expenses of a company. Even though companies often use cost structure to set their pricing and identify the areas with cost-saving potential (Gartner, 2024), this alone is not enough to define the real pricing nor saving potential. One of the known cost-saving methods that "blindly" utilizes single cost-saving potentials is the so-called cheese slicer method, in which expenditure cuts are done across the board to reach the total saving targets. These cuts may be simple to plan and execute (Berger, 2011), but they can very easily fall short of the saving targets or even turn into additional spending instead of actual saving. And the reason for this is the lack of understanding of interdependencies between different cost elements, leading very easily to saving in one aspect but doubling the expense on some other, leading to increased total costs. However, exactly the opposite result can be achieved with a full TCO analysis, in which different cost elements and the relationship between them are first analysed. This makes achieving the targeted savings much more probable, if not yet completely certain due to other variables related to cost-saving programs.

When talking about cost structure, the costs can also be divided into direct and indirect costs. The former can be quite easily attributed to a specific product, while the latter cannot, being formed, for example, by fixed costs of sales and marketing or management (Schmidt, 2015-2024). Often the direct costs are much easier to distinguish in the context of a certain product, which makes them visible costs in the TCO, while most indirect costs can easily remain hidden when thinking of total costs.

TCO brings a lot of benefits in the cost structure, many of which we shall discuss more in detail in Chapter 6, since they are related to corporate strategy and sales strategies. After all, for example, the financial situation of a company or its customer, and the political macro-environment of the company might dictate what kind of cost structure might be the most suitable in each case. Sometimes this restriction might be so strong that it overrules the best solution in terms of TCO, but still the full TCO analysis brings a lot of value even in these situations. Let's create an example:

A potential customer has approached a company, requesting a quotation for the manufacturing of their product. However, this company cannot pay the required investments upfront but has proposed amortizing 80% of the CAPEX into the piece price of manufactured products. In this situation, a TCO analysis becomes perhaps even more important to the potential supplier of this company, because calculating the costs of manufacturing plus the CAPEX amortization into it correctly will play a major role in the total profitability of this deal. And if this potential supplier is in a challenging financial position itself, the incorrect pricing can even make this company bankrupt. But as discussed, we shall elaborate upon this in further detail in Chapter 6. Additionally, understanding the connection between cost structure and TCO is important in cost calculations, or costing, as we shall discuss next.

3.2 Costing and TCO

Next, we shift our focus to cost calculations and costing in general. "Costing is a type of accounting that works to assess an organization's total cost of production by looking at both variable and fixed costs during each step of production." (Indeed Editorial Team, 2024). Proficiency in different methods of cost accounting is of great assist at cost calculation and pricing, which are important for the profitability of a business. There are several kinds of costing, each of which requires an understanding of its suitability for different purposes to get the correct picture of the total costs. These are much more extensively covered in management accounting literature and school classes on the topic, and I recommend studying this topic further if you, who are reading this book, find it interesting and/or important for your work or targets.

All these costing techniques bring value to TCO work, some to overall TCO, some to different cost elements in it. And of course, we mustn't forget the TCO of costing processes, either. They mustn't be overly expensive to implement and upkeep and, at the same time, they must be able to provide the required data to form a solid decision-making basis (Järvenpää et al., 2013, p. 121). For example, lifecycle costing is a highly useful tool for calculating the total cost of ownership in some respects, but this costing method alone does not form the total cost of ownership in most cases. The case is somewhat similar for target costing, which is mainly applied in the product development phase, during which most cost drivers are also formed; thus, also the biggest cost-saving potentials can be found during this phase. And that is why in this book there is an entire chapter dedicated to the topic of product development process and TCO.

This relationship between costing methods and TCO works also the other way around, in which TCO brings a lot of added value to costing work. After all, correct identification and monetisation of hidden costs is crucial to successful costing work. For example, in target costing the target price or planned features in the product might have to be re-evaluated if the TCO calculations show that with the planned selling price and planned features in the product the profit margin falls short of the target, or no profit is achieved at all.

And even though a big portion of cost savings can be achieved by optimizing the product design and manufacturing methods, there are also a lot of other factors where cost savings can be found, thus increasing the profit margin and/or giving the ability to lower the selling price, depending on the product strategy. These other factors are discussed in many points in this book, because they are often the hidden costs in product development and manufacturing, but when added up together, they have a major impact on the financial result for a single product and in the entire company.

This entire topic shall be discussed in further detail in Chapter 9, but next we shall discuss more useful parities between TCO and different management accounting terminology and their correct implementation.

3.3 Payback period and breakeven point & TCO

Payback period and breakeven point are both valid topics in TCO in many ways. The payback period is the time it takes to recover the cost of an investment (Kagan, 2024). In practice, the payback period can be defined either by the forecast of additional sales, and later verified with actualised additional sales, or with the calculation of how much OPEX can be saved with the onetime CAPEX investment. Let's illustrate this first with an example of application of TCO principles and then with application of TCO principles.

A company has decided to automate a part of the manufacturing process and requested the process engineer responsible for the respective production area to make the payback calculation for the investment. The engineer calculates the required investments to plan and execute this automation work. The calculations give 250 000 €, and the process engineer finds the investment profitable because this investment allows reducing the quantity of operators in this area by two, bringing annual wage savings of 140 000 €, thus giving a payback period of 1,79 years, which is roughly 1 year and 9 months. However, the same calculation done with the principles of TCO, which bring the focus to hidden costs and, on the other hand, hidden saving potentials, shows that aside from the process equipment and related software and hardware investments, investments are needed for the training of the production personnel, additional spare parts for the stock and electric connections for the equipment. This brings the total investment need to 295 000 €. Additionally, annual OPEX costs are increased by additional wear parts worth 1 500 € per year and increased maintenance need worth 700 € per year. On the other hand, this automatization also improves the quality output in this process area, which leads to the reduction of annual scrap costs by 5 000 € and annual rework costs by 11 200 €. With this information, the payback period is calculated as

$$\frac{295\ 000\ €}{(140\ 000 - 1500 - 700 + 5000 + 11\ 200\ )€} = 1,92\ years = 1\ year\ 11\ months.$$ Both payback

periods can be considered acceptable as long as the company has the funds required to pay for the needed investments, but this calculation demonstrates the importance of the total cost of ownership in this context. And this is only a simplified example. Aside from the mentioned cost elements, there can be other hidden costs or cost savings, such as:

➢ replacement of part racks designed for a manual process with ones designed for an automated process

➢ savings from reduced sick leaves

> savings or additional expenses for internal logistics when handling these different types of racks.

TCO is also very important in the definition of the break-even point. In practice, the break-even point is the volume of sold products that exactly covers all the expenses created by manufacturing the product and related activities (Järvenpää et al., 2013, p. 102). This calculation is one of the most important calculations when defining the potential profitability of a product, and that's why it is very important that this calculation is done correctly. Just like in the example of payback period, also here the principles of TCO can reveal hidden costs, as well as cost-saving potentials if modifying the production process. Sometimes the difference in break-even point with and without applying TCO can be small, if the overestimation of expenditure in the considered cost elements is sufficient to cover for the hidden costs, but the difference can also be very significant. It is not an enormous simplification to state that the closer to the maximum capacity the production must run to reach profitability, the more crucial this calculation becomes. For example:

The maximum annual capacity of the production process is 80 000 units per year. The initial calculation for the break-even point gave the result of 60 000 units, which was still considered reasonable by the top management during decision-making. However, when the same calculation was later done with the principles of TCO, it turned out that the break-even point is 73 000 units. This, combined with the fact that due to the variations in quality output and the productivity of the production process, led to a situation in which the company made a loss with the product every year. Being a mass product, with no multiple other products being produced at the same time, the company launched a cost-saving campaign.

3.4   Cash flow and decision making & TCO

From payback period and breakeven point, we switch to the next monetary view of TCO: cash flow and financial decision-making. Cash flow is net cash and equivalents being transferred in and out of a company (Hayes, 2024). Basically, there are two major elements in cash flow forecasts: the sums of money and their timing in the calendar, both of which benefit greatly from TCO. Total cost of ownership and related calculations and identification of potential hidden costs can improve the accuracy of cash flow forecasting immensely in multiple ways. Identification of potential hidden costs reduces the risk of sudden negative surprises in the cash flow forecast as increased utility and wear part consumption or increased packaging costs due to changes in the product, for example. Additionally, there are multiple types of cost elements among potential hidden costs, which means their correct identification will improve the accuracy of the cash flow forecasting both in the sums of money and timing. On the other hand, these hidden costs can add up to even immense sums of money, which could have a major impact on the profitability of a project, for example. And if these impacts are faced as a surprise, with very little time to react, this could potentially mean substantial challenges in the overall finances of a company. This is why it is crucial that the cash flow forecasting contains these important pieces of information for financial decision-making as early as possible.

The financial decision-making in a company is based on the information provided by the finance department and financial reports used in the company. These decision-making situations are related to the planning, guiding and monitoring of the corporate activities, including topics like:

➢ investments
➢ recruitments
➢ pricing
➢ marketing campaigns
➢ supplier selection
➢ strategy work and
➢ process development (Järvenpää et al., 2013, pp. 36-38).

Each of these situations includes a great variety of cost elements of different natures with very different related costs. However, TCO is very applicable to each of these because the accuracy of the forecasts concerning the financial effects of choices between different options can be improved greatly with a good understanding of Total Cost of Ownership, as described above. This way, the top management can have more reliable and more timely financial data to use as a basis for the decision-making process, which has great potential to lead to better strategic choices and improved profitability. And, as we shall discuss further in Chapter 8, this profitability improvement is often much more sustainable than what can be achieved with intentions of temporary cost savings, such as layoffs.

3.5   Budgeting and TCO

A budget is a monetised plan of activities that aims for an excellent result. The budget is created in a planned and guided process that is called budgeting, and it is vital for long-term planning and for the aim of trying to achieve the strategic goals.

The purposes of budgeting are:

- ➢ setting targets and communicating about them
- ➢ resource allocation
- ➢ organisational development and coordination
- ➢ delegating the decision-making mandate and clarifying the areas of responsibility
- ➢ guiding the profitability, liquidity and solvency
- ➢ enhancing operational efficiency
- ➢ performance evaluation of the management
- ➢ encouraging the people in the organisation and
- ➢ securing the financial future of the company (Järvenpää et al., 2013, p. 235–236).

There are several aspects and phases in the budgeting process:

- ➢ overhead budget, e.g.
  - o general management
  - o accounting and legal
  - o support functions
- ➢ sales budget, e.g.
  - o purchase orders
  - o sales forecasts
- ➢ marketing budget, allocated in stuff like
  - o marketing campaigns
  - o company brand
- ➢ warehousing budget, allocated for warehousing of e.g.
  - o raw materials and components
  - o assemblies and sub-assemblies
- ➢ manufacturing budget, which includes for example
  - o personnel costs
  - o budgeted manufacturing volume
  - o manufacturing overheads
- ➢ investment budget for the planned investments
- ➢ purchasing budget, which includes e.g.
  - o components and raw materials
  - o indirect materials (Järvenpää et al, 2013, p. 240).

These budgets provide to and receive input from each other, forming first the sub-budgets and then the main budgets of a company, the latter of which are budgeted financial result, funding budget and budgeted balance sheet (Järvenpää et al., 2013, p. 240).

It is also very important to understand these budgets in the context of Total Cost of Ownership. After all, these budgets define the funds available for each function to achieve the targeted overall financial result, which has a major impact on what kind of cost structure would be ideal to either get even or under the budget in each function. In an ideal situation, TCO is applied already during the budgeting process, and in related planning, increasing the probability of the outcome in which the resulting budgets will match the actual needs of the company both in sums of money and timing as well as possible. Of course, there is always some degree of uncertainty related to estimating and forecasting the future, and this means even with the application of TCO the actual needs of funds both in sums and timing can differ from the originally planned and budgeted figures, so even that does not "fix" that uncertainty. However, without TCO application in the budgeting phase, there is a much greater chance of mistakes both in sums of money and timing, as well as neglecting some cost elements completely, as described in previous sections of this book. In other words, with successful application of TCO in budgeting, there will be a greatly reduced risk of unpleasant surprises as expenses that were previously unaccounted for in related budgets, estimates and forecasts. And even if the original budget hasn't been created in combination with TCO, the overall financial result can still be achieved according to the originally planned budget. However, especially when talking about a budget concerning cross-functional stakeholders, this often requires that these stakeholders prioritise the common goal of the budget over their respective sub-budgets per function. And this is much more likely to happen in a high-performing organisation that works well together towards one common goal instead of a siloed organisation in which teams make decisions solely based on how these decisions affect single teams and single individuals within them. But these topics will be discussed further in Chapter 8. Next, we will shift our focus to the main aim of TCO work, increasing profitability.

3.6   Profitability and TCO

Being the ultimate goal of TCO, this could work well as the summary for the complete book, or we could even end our journey here. But just like Columbus didn't arrive in the Americas by turning home after entering the Atlantic Ocean, we won't understand the full potential of TCO if we finish here. So instead, let's focus on why it is important to understand the connection between TCO and profitability. After all, successful TCO work has great potential to improve the profitability of a company significantly. Unlike the cheese-slicer method, as previously discussed, TCO aims at understanding the interdependence between different cost elements throughout the product lifecycle and related functions and activities in them, as well as decisions made. This in turn enables taking cost-saving measures that improve profitability. This does not mean profit cannot be made without the application of TCO, but it has great potential to improve the profitability significantly and sustainably. As we shall discuss in the later chapters, for example in chapters 4 and 8, there are multiple ways to improve the profitability of daily routine operations without major investments or resorting to temporary layoffs, which rarely lead to the targeted level of cost savings as we shall discuss more in detail in Chapter 8.

Why do improving profitability and TCO go hand in hand to create a positive cycle within a company, then? Successful implementation of TCO not only increases the overall profitability of a company, but it also requires a lot of collaboration between functions and departments to identify all relevant cost elements and to optimize the related costs. This helps departments build bridges between them, thus improving overall collaboration, which makes working together more efficient. TCO also has a great potential to improve the financial performance of single functions, which might be one of the bonus payment criteria for the directors of functions. Even though this might motivate these directors to increase their mutual collaboration, personally I would discourage this kind of bonus criteria as in many cases it has a greater chance of reducing collaboration for the benefit of the whole company rather than increasing it, as we shall discuss further in the chapter 8.

Another aspect of this positive cycle is that the successful identification of all cost elements often engages a lot of experts in different fields of work. On the other hand, increased profitability improves the chances of a company to survive even the most challenging times (Jansson, 2018). Increased profitability also reduces the pressure to lay off people temporarily if these increased profits are not solely making the owners even richer, meaning all the increased profit would be given out as dividends, for example.

3.7   Cost trends and TCO

With the major inflation of the past three years, having started in the summer 2021 (Eurostat, 2024), following up the cost trends has become increasingly important for the profitability of businesses. A company that buys a lot of the same materials and components annually or even more frequently has a good chance of staying on track of the historical cost development of these materials and components by systematically documenting and following up these trends. And for many common goods, such as crude oil, there are forecasts available online, even with different scenarios related to different forecasted cost trends.

However, in a company that, for example, does a big project every few years or even less frequently, it is crucial to follow-up these cost trends and forecasts not only outside the projects but also during them (author's experience). This helps in many aspects of cost engineering work in the company, such as improving the accuracy of financial estimates and forecasts during an extensive project and staying on track of the unit costs of goods and services required to complete a project. And since we live in the age of global competition, understanding these trends on the domestic market won't suffice. A global understanding is required for many purposes, such as:

- ➢ investigating cost saving opportunities
- ➢ planning the production locations
- ➢ understanding if the supplier pricing is justified
- ➢ how to time the purchases of raw material and components
    - ○ does the company have a chance for a relatively high volatility of stock?
    - ○ does enabling this bring in more costs than what is saved by timing the purchases of huge volumes with low market prices?
- ➢ supplier contracts; how to consider the big changes in raw material and component costs in the pricing agreements
- ➢ quotation calculations; having unit prices of the goods and services up to date during the calculation phase, mitigating the risk of major over- or under-pricing.

All in all, cost trends are a crucial topic to TCO, especially in the purchases where a major share of costs comes from energy, as can be seen in Eurostat graphs (Eurostat, 2024).

3.8   Pricing and customer quotations & TCO

Pricing and customer quotations are one of the elements of profitability in business. Pricing affects the revenue directly, and thus also profitability, which is why it is crucial to have the correct understanding of the total cost level, too. After all, the revenue must exceed the costs for a company to be profitable (Järvenpää et al., 2013, pp. 212-213). There are multiple different pricing methods, such as:

> cost-based pricing

> market-based pricing

> target pricing

> value-based pricing and

> agreed price.

All these pricing methods benefit greatly from successful TCO work, because it helps the company to understand how it should price its products to be profitable. This, combined with the correct understanding of the price level on the market, tells if the company is working at the correct cost level to be profitable.

Besides pricing, specific customer quotations are also crucial to the profitability of a company. What kind of cost elements are included depends on the complexity of the work scope being quoted, field and type of work and many other aspects, such as if it will be the buyer or the seller who will own the assets upon installation and commissioning in industrial projects, for example. However, regardless of these aspects, the TCO elements in quotation calculations are almost always, if not always, both monetary and non-monetary. Monetary elements may include topics such as:

> unit cost of personnel wages and total workload required

> unit and total cost estimations of OPEX and CAPEX

> unit cost of manufacturing

> scenarios related to each if the potential customer has not yet defined the production volumes, for example.

Non-monetary elements of TCO may include topics such as:

> payment steps and related criteria and payment terms

> delivery terms, INCOTERMS

> information available during the time of the quotation calculation

> assumptions made when the needed information is not available

> legal aspects and contract clauses

> organisation working both on the quotation process as well as in the resulting project

> the scope of work agreed with the customer (author's experience) and

> what this agreed external scope of work means in the internal scope of work, meaning what is the correct work breakdown structure (WBS) to complete this external scope of work (Hermarij, 2021, p. 35).

TCO can help with this work in multiple ways, both in understanding the full scope of work and cost elements as well as finding and utilizing cost-saving opportunities. With the help of regular follow-up of cost trends, the current and potential future unit costs can be estimated or calculated more accurately, while understanding the TCO elements of each aspect of the work scope provides crucial information both for cost calculations and resource planning. For example, if the project being quoted involves a lot of process equipment and surrounding hardware, such as automation, that a company hasn't used in its production process previously, it typically is very useful to have a maintenance expert in the project organisation starting in very early stages of the project. But in the means of resourcing, focusing only on the project at the expense of the quotation calculation phase is not enough. The more complex the work scope, the more experts in different fields of work should be involved already in the quotation calculation phase. This will be well worth the expense and effort even if the quotation does not lead to a contract, because every quotation team member learns something new from every quotation case. And this knowledge can prove to be vital later in some other project. Aside from the learning curve, a quotation calculation team that is well suited for the work scope being quoted can find a lot of cost saving potentials already during the quotation calculation work and understand the work breakdown structure in full, thus reducing the costs and improving the profitability throughout the whole product lifecycle belonging to the scope being quoted. If the company lacks the knowledge required to estimate the pricing of some element in the WBS, it might also be worthwhile to hire temporarily an external consultant who is an expert on that precise element.

Besides the direct and indirect cost elements related to the project and product itself, the quotation process is its own cost element. The bigger and more complex the work scope in the quotation phase and the project or product being quoted are, the more important it is to have a standardised approach to the quotation process itself. Aside from engineering work and quotation calculations, the steps of this process may include:

> internal mid-term reviews with key stakeholders

> confirming the feasibility of the assumptions made

> regular updates of related data if more data is received during the quotation process.

In general, a well-structured quotation process improves the fluency of work at this phase. And this often shows in the quality of quotation work, which gives the first impression to the potential customer and the customer's purchasing representative (author's experience). And this process-oriented ending of this chapter guides us towards the next chapter, Working process efficiency and TCO.

4   WORKING PROCESS EFFICIENCY AND TCO

Next, we shift our focus to what doesn't seem to be very well covered in the literature and online sources on the topic of TCO: working process efficiency. Improving the cost effectiveness of working processes in the office work is something easily overlooked. After all, managing to save 100 000 € or even more on one purchase throughout its lifetime is much more concrete than, for example, saving 100 000 € in a year by rationalising meeting and reporting routines. The principles of value engineering and value analysis, as discussed in Chapter 2, can be utilized also here: Can we achieve the same functionality with less cost or improve the functionality while retaining the current cost level?

As you, dear reader, might have observed in the table of contents of this book, this chapter is quite long, but so is the topic. Aside from the sources listed along this chapter and in the list of sources at the end of this book, the contents of this chapter are based on my experience of 9 years at project work. Thus, many of the viewpoints in this chapter are from the "project world" but applicable in any office work, of course always considering the environment and conditions where these principles are aimed to be applied. During these 9 years I have made a lot of observations on the office work and studied leadership and organisational sciences. And for this reason, for anyone willing to understand this aspect of TCO further, aside from TCO itself, I highly recommend studying leadership and organisational sciences, as well as value engineering and value analysis.

4.1   Measure thrice, cut once – Process TCO through planning

When I was in my early 20s, I used to watch a lot of car programs. In one of them, The Wheeler Dealers (no sponsorship nor paid advertising, just a memory), the mechanic would say, "measure thrice, cut once". The same principle applies to planning, especially in more complex cases. In IPMA, the project plan is defined as "the plan that describes the deliverables, their budget, their durations and their quality requirements" (Hermarij, 2021, p. 183). And here lies the first potential challenge of a project: If this viewpoint is wrongly interpreted and adopted in the organisation as the leading thought, that each responsibility area would have its own duration, own deliverables, own budget and own quality requirements without the interdependence between different areas of responsibility, the resulting ways of working would be very siloed. However, as previously described, the interdependencies between these responsibility areas can be illustrated, for example, with a Work Breakdown Structure. I recommend emphasizing this mutually dependent relationship between the responsibility areas wherever this emphasis is fluent to be attached, such as the project master schedule. As we shall discuss later in this chapter, siloed ways of working are one of the biggest hindrances to the successful TCO work.

In the context of a project lifecycle, planning is the phase during which biggest cost effects are created in the eyes of the project, if not always in the eyes of the entire company. And even though focusing on the project goes in some sense against the whole point of TCO, these are not two opposite things. After all, if a company has a separate project organisation responsible for the setting, planning and execution of the projects, it is vital for the entire company that this organisation understands the TCO effects of its decisions. Moreover, the investigations required for successful TCO work also guide the thinking of the people in project organisation to identify all the relevant cost elements that they affect directly.

The planning phase consists of many activities, such as:

➢ creating the full project plan based on an initial version that was hopefully created during the project setting phase

➢ creating the full project master time schedule, the same comment applies as above

➢ setting up the routines to fulfil the requirements of the project, derived from customer requirements and internal guidelines

➢ creating first concepts of the deliverables

➢ many kinds of related planning, all of which is crucial to the success of the project.

All these aspects of planning require considering the relevant key stakeholders for each topic, as well as planning all relevant activities well ahead. This saves time, money and nerves of the whole organisation by reducing the risk of sudden negative surprises, reducing the number of conflicts resulting from poor decisions made under enormous pressure and reducing the risk of delay in the project timeline. Good planning done well ahead also has great potential to affect the supplier relations positively by enabling the suppliers a reasonable amount of time to plan and execute their work correctly. And all these benefits yield positive TCO results. A smart organisation also implements its documented lessons learned from previous projects in all plans. This way, the implementation of best practices and avoidance of the worst mistakes should not depend on whether the project personnel has worked in the previous projects in the company or not.

4.1.1 Scheduling

Scheduling is one of the most challenging and one of the most important aspects of complex projects. A good project master schedule contains:

1. deliverables
2. tasks
3. task start and end dates
4. task dependencies
5. project calendar
6. work packages
7. task duration and project timeline
8. budgets
9. resource availability
10. schedule risk analysis (ProjectManager.com, 2024).

This list is from a webpage of a scheduling software provider, and I have never used this software, so I do not know if the software itself is good or not. However, the points listed are very valid; the budgets may be handled using other methods in the project, but all other points stand. And in TCO, based on my own observations, I would like to highlight three items on the list: task dependencies, resource availability and schedule risk analysis. The first of these three, task dependencies, has great power to help the whole project organisation understand how the work of each organisation member affects and is dependent on the work done by colleagues in the same organisation. This has an enormous impact on the collaboration towards one common goal, as we shall discuss further in Chapter 8. Secondly, the resource availability is another crucial TCO point in the project schedule. After all, typically it is cheaper to complete the project utilizing the regular working time with minimal overtime by anyone. This, of course, is not always possible if the project has been sold with too tight a timeline and there aren't enough people to do the work in the regular working time. However, in my point of view this is more of an expense than saving, because continuous overtime not only increases direct wage costs as overtime fees but also increases the mental load placed on the shoulders of each member of the organisation, increasing the tendency of making mistakes (Rian & Disman, 2023), thus even further increasing the overall workload in the project by requiring more working time to correctly complete each part of the work scope. This might lead to a situation where some important tasks are pushed forward in time, which creates even more pressure towards the organisation and the vicious cycle is ready to ruin the entire project and lead to several burnouts.

Lastly, it is equally important to understand the schedule risk. After all, reading the planned task start dates and deadlines without understanding the important concepts of Critical Path and Total Slack might lead to chaos in which everything is equally important, nothing is prioritised, and nothing is completed with good quality. John Hermarij in his IPMA work defines Critical Path as "the longest sequence of activities to be carried out in a (part of a) time schedule and Total Slack as "the total amount of time by which an activity can be delayed, without increasing the project duration" (Hermarij, 2021, p. 58). Both concepts are also important TCO points in office working processes, because understanding these topics helps the whole project organisation to work efficiently and complete its work to a good quality in the given timeline, if the timeline was reasonable to begin with.

4.1.2 Budgeting and cost control & TCO

Budgeting and cost control are another vital TCO aspect of project work. In this context, budgeting can be quite different from the methods introduced in Chapter 3.5. In extensive projects, there are a few main budgets forming one total figure. These budgets are then divided over all sub-projects within the same project, forming, for example, personnel workload budget, project cost budget and investment budget of one sub-project. Financial estimates are then made throughout the project both in sums of money and in timing to forecast if there will be a budget overrun or under-run and how the spending of money will be divided over the project timeline.

And herein lies the first potential "threat" to successful TCO optimisation in this context: If the rewarding of the project personnel is based on these single sub-budgets and their corresponding estimates, this combined with certain types of personality (Robbins & Judge, 2022, p. 197) might result in a very siloed and very individualistic behaviour, which often causes more additional expenses than savings. On the other hand, a good understanding of the TCO of the goods and services required to fulfil the scope of the project enables us to split these initial budgets so that they would respond to the needs of each responsibility area as well as possible. However, there are certain restrictions on how freely we can reallocate the budget once the initial budget is confirmed. These restrictions can be related to, for example, internal company guidelines and the ownership of the completed product or production process. The easiest starting point for this is a company owning the assets once completed and internal guidelines enabling reallocating the budget quite freely as long as sticking to the approved total of that sub-budget. And to promote good collaboration within the project team, this reallocation should be done in collaboration between the leaders of each responsibility area. Even though this way of working will increase the number of attendees in a few meetings quite significantly, it increases the commitment of each responsibility area to the commonly agreed budget and otherwise enhances collaboration, both of which have positive effects on overall TCO. The source of this positive effect comes from the feeling of procedural justice, "the perceived fairness of the process" (Robbins & Judge, 2022, p. 141). In addition to the huge potential it has to improve the accuracy of financial forecasts in the project, TCO may provide vital chances to make further technical improvements than originally planned while still staying within the agreed budget, which very likely reduces the operating costs later in the product lifecycle. On the other hand, TCO can also be utilized in payback period calculations to show that even if the financial forecast of the project already shows overrun compared to budget, some certain investments can still be very sensible to make, even if they were not originally included in the project scope, or, if not defined in the project scope, omitted for example from the delivery scope of suppliers. This can be the case, for example, for some simple rework or quality control equipment that doesn't cost dozens of thousands but saves a lot of working time monthly and even more annually. If some highly useful investment was not in the original scope, personally I would recommend payback period calculation for its simplicity to evaluate if it would still be worth it to invest in such equipment. However, to make the payback period calculation accurate, TCO principles must be applied.

In projects, and in business budgeting goes hand in hand with cost control. A few aspects should guide the strictness of cost control:

- ➢ what is the overall financial forecast of the whole project compared to the overall budget ➜ overrun or under-run?
- ➢ what are the project strategy and company strategy?
- ➢ what is the overall financial status of the company?
- ➢ do the proposed purchases bring in additional cost savings elsewhere ➜ what is the total monetary effect?
- ➢ is the current project scope still the same as it was at the time of defining the budget?

> ➢ has the change management been conducted correctly in the project, meaning have all the changes coming from customer's direction outside the original scope of the project been treated as additional sales (Ranganath, 2024)?

However, whatever is the case with each of these aspects, just like TCO, the cost controlling should be viewed comprehensively. After all, in a project all the personnel get paid for delivering the whole project. It will not benefit anyone in the big picture if some responsibility areas complete their work within the given timeline and budget at the expense of some other responsibility areas, and even more so if this expense in one area is greater than the saving in another. Equally little benefit is gained if the purchases in one responsibility area are limited due to budget overrun if the overall financial forecast is still well below the budget. This will only create unnecessary friction and conflict within the project organisation, hindering the work in the entire project and, in some worst cases, even failing the project altogether, or at least delaying it. And with the sanction fees of failure or delay of the end of project timeline can exceed the additional expenses from overruns in single responsibility areas many times over. This is why the approach to cost control can be a very sensitive topic in general, which is why common and commonly understood guidelines should be created for this purpose in the company (author's experience).

4.1.3 Project kick-off and TCO

John Hermarij in his IPMA work defines Kick-Off as a "meeting at the commencement of the project, or a stage in the project, to stimulate an effective and efficient execution of the project or stage" (Hermarij, 2021). However, at this point I want to add: Effective and efficient do not mean the same as getting to work without proper preparation and planning. A badly executed kick-off can have catastrophic effects on the morale of the project organisation by:

> ➢ leaving the project scope and deliverables unclear
> ➢ not providing sufficient insight into various aspects of the project
> ➢ leaving the project team unaware of the key stakeholders of each responsibility area
> ➢ in general, leaving the project team to figure out on their own what and how they should do in the project (Ruslanova, 2024).

This and more is everything that a well-executed kick-off will not result in. And aside from these aspects, a kick-off also has a major psychological impact. The kick-off is typically held by the project manager and/or the sub-project manager, and even though we all are adults, human mind tends to follow the example of the leaders (Robbins & Judge, 2022, p. 146). In practice, this means that a well-executed kick-off has a great chance to make the project team highly motivated to do their work well, with good quality and fluent collaboration with each other, while a badly executed kick-off can have the opposite impact, showing the project manager doesn't value the impact that the kick-off might have on the team and that it is just a "necessary evil to get out of the way". For example, I often feel great excitement about the start of a new project, and I can sense it in my colleagues, too. However, this excitement and eagerness to get to work might get crushed if the attitude towards its start shown by the leader is "whatever" (author's experience).

4.2   Resourcing, personnel and TCO

The next point about working processes in the office is resourcing. Basically, this entire section is based on the idea of choosing the lowest total cost overall over the whole organisation instead of the lowest unit cost plus how the personnel planning and resource planning can be done. However, I want to make a distinction between resources and personnel, because we people differ from other resources. We are living, breathing and thinking beings with emotions, values and needs. As taught in the study of business ethics (Crane et al., 2019, p. 291), according to Kantian theory we should always treat humanity "always as an end and never as a means only". After all, humans deserve to be respected and to have certain basic rights. Which is why we shall use the words personnel, people, etc. of the people working in a company instead of the word resource. When it comes to people in the organisation, in this chapter we shall focus on the aspects of competence, collaboration and sufficiency. Other human aspects we shall discuss in further detail in the Chapter 8. On the other hand, there are also non-human things needed to achieve the goals of the organization, typically non-living, and of these we shall use the word resource.

When forming a project organisation, there are several considerations to be made. Ultimately, there are three groups of people in a project organisation: permanent organisation, third party and freelancers (Hermarij, 2021, p. 147), of whom the representatives of third party and freelancers are hired temporarily for the duration of a project or of one or more of its phases. The people from the permanent organisation are internal personnel, whereas third party and freelancer personnel are external. In the strategic personnel plan (strategic resource plan in the source) the following items are described:

- ➢ The required personnel and how they are introduced to the team.
- ➢ The different procedures applicable to internal and external personnel.
- ➢ When these people are needed, and how will they return to their respective departments or organisations.
- ➢ If there are people working part time, a summary of their work schedules is needed.
- ➢ "Any other applicable restrictions on their employment."
- ➢ The training needed for the personnel to acquire the knowledge and skills needed in the project.
- ➢ The applicable laws in place and how to comply with them.
- ➢ Principles of rewarding exceptional performance and how to let the line organisation managers know about it (Hermarij, 2021, p. 148).

Additionally, the personnel plan in a project should contain the planned monthly workload and the role of each team member. This brings clarity to, for example, the situations of rearranging the organisation and when a person leaves the team in the middle of the project, showing directly which role is left temporarily vacant.

In the context of TCO, it is often a mistake to just "stare" at the unit wage cost of this personnel. If prioritising the cheapest option available that can barely manage the required tasks, we might very easily end up with a team that doesn't work well together, thus adding up to the total number of working hours consumed in the project, which eats up the savings that were tried to be achieved by resorting to the cheapest unit wage cost. Since there are a lot of different tasks and activities required to complete a complex project, different people with different skill sets are needed, too (author's experience). And this brings diversity to the team. Personally, I find this good, although this requires a lot of consideration for different ways of handling conflicts (Browaeys & Price, 2019, p. 406) and, for example, differences in focus on relationship or task-orientation in different culture (Mujtaba, 2008), especially if these people come from different regions.

In general, from the viewpoint of TCO optimization, it is best to have competent project personnel that works well together and can get the tasks at hand completed in the schedule and on the first try with good quality. Of course, we are all human and we all make mistakes, but continuous rework and the added pressure from it are still more expensive than agreeing to pay the higher unit wage cost. That said, high unit wage cost alone does not guarantee excellent performance, but it is still more common to get a competent project team member with a higher unit wage cost than with a lower one. After all, for example, 1 500 h x 60 €/h is less than

3 000 h x 40 €/h for the same effort. And this calculation example does not include overtime fees etc. to catch up with the schedule.

Similar logic applies to the non-human resources, such as software and physical tools being used. The principles of TCO can be applied to these also separately, often showing that overall TCO is, in fact, lower for the software and tools sufficient for the purpose, even with a higher purchase price or rental cost, because they save so much time, nerves and money of the whole organisation. Which is why, if this software and tools are fit for purpose in all crucial ways, it often makes more sense to invest in good quality instead of the cheapest alternative, unless this cheapest alternative can still fulfil sufficient share of the use cases while not requiring a lot of extra work that would offset the cost savings from the purchase and operation cost differences. Additionally, successful resource management brings a multitude of positives to a project, such as increased profitability, more accurate timelines and estimates and increased employee morale (Indeed Editorial Team, 2024).

4.3   Meetings and reporting & TCO

Meetings and reporting — the eternal topic of debate in projects. Some say there are too few meetings; some find there are too many. And there are also many opinions about how a meeting should be run to keep it effective. Some prefer just getting it "over with" while others want to go through every single detail that sometimes is very loosely related to the agenda, even if this means the meeting end is delayed. Sometimes these descriptions of different approaches to a meeting are exaggerated, but there are also people who represent these viewpoints quite accurately. And the same goes for reporting, which can be done in many ways. And even though project management can play a major role in both aspects, often the reporting routines stem even more from the needs, wishes and demands of the middle-and upper management. However, there are universal ways to streamline both meetings and reporting routines. But even though these principles of streamlining are universal, their exact applicationwill they will always depend on how they fit the environment and conditions they are being applied in: The project status compared to plans, corporate culture and the needs and preferences of the organisation (author's experience).

As in many cases in working process efficiency, the principles of value engineering and value analysis apply here, too, meaning lowering the cost while maintaining the same functionality or improving functionality while maintaining the same cost. In the context of meetings and reporting, these costs are typically working hours spent in meetings and preparing and presenting reports. And these working hours must be multiplied by the number of people spending the time in these meetings and making reports to understand the related total cost.

In general, there are certain principles that define when arranging a meeting is required. These include, for example, the need for team building, the purpose of every attendee getting the new information urgently at the same time and the need for mutual communication back and forth. Additionally, the correct participants also need to be kept in mind when planning the meeting. Other crucial considerations in preparation for a meeting are:

➢ objective of the meeting

➢ subjects included in discussion

➢ correct people in correct roles to be invited

➢ creating a scheduled agenda and sending it out to the participants beforehand

➢ who is the chairman and who will write down the meeting minutes

➢ time and location of the meeting and related requirements.

During and after the meeting the key considerations are:

➢ respecting those who arrived on time by starting the meeting on time

➢ sticking to the agenda with a controlled point when to bring topics outside the agenda to the table

➢ actions list and related follow-up suitable for the meeting

➢ clear and precise minutes of meeting and distributing them to the attendees afterwards (Hermarij, 2021, pp. 454-457), in which precision means all key information, made decisions, mutually agreed measures and possible disagreements to these are documented.

Following these principles helps in having a full focus on the topics at hand in the meetings (author's experience).

Reporting is also another aspect that someone always finds a pain point. And it can be exactly that if every manager and director wants to define their own format in which they want the reporting to be done. However, it is much better in many ways to utilize the existing reports and their combinations as far as possible. Not only is this a more economical and efficient way to achieve the objectives of reporting, but it also reduces the feeling of frustration experienced by the project personnel in preparing the reports and frees up working hours for other purposes (author's experience). Good ways to streamline reporting are:

1. defining clear objectives and questions to guide data analysis and reporting

2. utilizing automated data analysis tools

3. developing and standardising reporting templates

4. clear visualisation of the data

5. using advanced analytics platforms (Lastiri, 2023).

And there are a lot of benefits of a good reporting management system. These benefits include:

➤ increased communication throughout the organisation

➤ improved productivity

➤ improved efficiency and decision-making

➤ early identification of potential problems, allowing more reaction time and

➤ enhanced return on investment (Elyea, 2023).

And even if a company has no chance to implement automated tools, already the clear guidance of data analysis and reporting, developing and standardising reporting templates and their use and developing clear visualisations of data in them has a huge potential to save time, money and everyone's nerves on reporting. And even if a new type of reporting need arises, in many cases the template for these new reports can be derived from another existing report instead of creating it from scratch (author's experience).

And one more piece of advice as a summary of this section: a good starting point to streamline meeting routines and reporting is to avoid having meetings and reports for the sake of meetings and reports. Both must always serve a valid purpose.

4.4   Coordination and documentation & TCO

Coordination and documentation are important to the success of a project. And the more complex the project is, the more significant these are for the success of a project. Successful coordination and clear and well-arranged documentation increase clarity, thus reducing the number of working hours of trying to figure out what was decided, by whom and who is responsible (author's experience).

John Hermarij in his IPMA work defines the role of coordinator (or chair) as someone who sees the big picture and helps others focus on their tasks (Hermarij, 2021, p. 440). The primary tasks of a project coordinator consist of supporting the project manager by overseeing administrative activities, communicating with different stakeholders and making sure the needed resources are available (Bridges, 2023). Thus, successful project coordination brings a lot of added value. Some of the key benefits of good project coordination include:

- ➢ increased awareness of the areas of importance and priority
- ➢ streamlined communication
- ➢ increasing the productivity and quality of the project
- ➢ helping the project stay within the schedule and budget and
- ➢ enhanced risk mitigation (Indeed Editorial Team, 2024).

All of these are also very important elements in the TCO. After all, improved productivity brings in more profit, while improved quality promotes improved customer satisfaction and customer loyalty (Fatma & Kumar, 2024).

Clear, precise and well-managed documentation also brings a lot of added value to any work in business. The more complex the topic or the project is, the more emphasis must be put on this point. After all, there are few as unnecessarily wasted working hours as those spent pointlessly searching for the documents that are not there, or time spent finally finding a document in a folder path completely disconnected from the topic and the purpose of the documentation.

In a project, everyone is usually responsible for documenting own work. On top of that, the project coordinator oversees the documentation and its management. Clear and well-structured project documentation:

- ➢ helps in project planning
- ➢ enhances project status follow-up and communication
- ➢ improves risk management
- ➢ puts governance in place
- ➢ makes project traceable
- ➢ enhances resource planning and assignment
- ➢ helps the team to focus on what's important
- ➢ makes it easier to incorporate changes (PanLearn, 2024).

And speaking of changes, have you, the reader of this book, ever been in a project organisation in which there are a lot of newcomers? In such a project, good documentation of the past is vital for the newcomers to understand the ways of working, what's been accomplished so far and what has been agreed internally within the whole project organisation and what has been agreed externally with the customer. If the documentation of these aspects either doesn't exist or is very unclear in structure or form, the newcomers are left with no choice than to either rely on the introduction hopefully received from the more experienced team members or to figure things out on their own. And this learning will take time, containing learning through trial and error and discovering things one at the time. And this could have been avoided with the combination of a proper introduction to the project, clear and well-structured documentation and proactivity of both the newcomers and their more experienced colleagues.

4.5   Change management and TCO

Change is always inevitable in this volatile world. This also applies to work in business, for example in complex industrial projects. There are also other types of change management, but in this section, we shall focus on managing scope changes in the project and engineering changes of the product and their connection to TCO.

It is not very uncommon for the delivery scope of a project to change "on the go", in the middle of the project. And this is fine if there is a logical process in place to handle such situations (author's experience). However, there are a variety of things to consider with the changes in the scope of the project:

- ➢ What was originally agreed scope?
- ➢ Why has this change occurred; was it on our or customer's initiative?
- ➢ What exactly is the addition to the project scope?
- ➢ Do we have sufficient personnel in quantity and competence to execute this change?
  - ○ If not, can we get these people from our own permanent organisation or shall we need third party or freelancer help temporarily?
- ➢ Do we have the technology required to execute this change?
  - ○ If not, can we source this technology and do we have the capability and space to install it and competence to operate it?
- ➢ Who are the stakeholders affected by this change? How are they affected?
- ➢ What has been agreed with the customer about project scope changes in general?

These are vital questions when calculating the costs of the scope change for the purposes of the quotation upon the topic, which will have an impact on the profitability of this additional scope and TCO through correct definition of cost elements involved. Additionally, it will be much easier for the project organisation to adapt to this change if a logical process is in place and it is utilised in the correct manner (author's experience).

Besides scope change management, especially projects involving a medium to low product maturity may contain a lot of engineering changes to the product. As with the project scope change management, having a logical process in place will work wonders here as well, even though it alone does not ensure the success. These engineering changes must be documented well including what has been changed, what is the new revision of the changed part or assembly, incorporating these changes in all the documents including product data with revision history and was the change made on seller's or buyer's initiative, because in many cases the last point defines if the change can be a subject to additional sales in the project or not. On the other hand, also the changes made on the seller's initiative can be a subject to additional sales, if at least a part of the product design is in the seller's scope of work. In such a case, the total cost of ownership for both may even remain on a similar level as before the change, but, for example, the cost structure between OPEX and CAPEX is altered.

And even though doing all these process steps might seem like a lot of work, it will still be less effort and less cost to complete them properly instead of not doing so, leading to a situation where nobody knows what was changed, why and how. This might very easily lead to a situation in which the additional sales based on these changes will lose all credibility (author's experience). In this situation, the costs will remain for the seller to bear, but the seller will not get any additional funds from the buyer, thus affecting the profitability of the entire company negatively. And if not having the discipline to conduct thorough change management and doing so consistently, in the worst case it might even lead to the bankruptcy of the company.

And even if a company has no chance to implement automated tools, already the clear guidance of data analysis and reporting, developing and standardising reporting templates and their use and developing clear visualisations of data in them has a huge potential to save time, money and everyone's nerves on reporting. And even if a new type of reporting need arises, in many cases the template for these new reports can be derived from another existing report instead of creating it from scratch (author's experience).

And one more piece of advice as a summary of this section: a good starting point to streamline meeting routines and reporting is to avoid having meetings and reports for the sake of meetings and reports. Both must always serve a valid purpose.

4.6   Data & TCO

Last, but not least for this chapter, we come to the enormous topic of data. But do not worry, dear Reader, I shall limit the topic in this book to keep a focus on the very basics of data and its relationship with TCO. After all, there are vast amounts of different kinds of data, such as price data, engineering data, production data and so on. There seem to be some further studies on the topic available, so if you would like to get to know this topic in further detail, I highly recommend doing so. In this section we shall focus mainly on two kinds of data: engineering data and price data.

Engineering data includes all the technical information needed for a specific project. These contain things such as 2D drawings and 3D models and other product data and operation and maintenance manuals of the process equipment (Law Insider, 2013-2024). All this data is very important in industrial projects. And that this data exists is not enough. It also needs to be correct in form, information and structure. If not, a lot of valuable working hours and additional monetary expenses are wasted on rework in pretty much all the technical areas of project execution (author's experience). Poor data quality can lead to bad decision-making, reduce productivity and profitability, reduce customer satisfaction and retention and increase business risks (Hawker, 2023), all of which create additional expenses, reducing profitability. And this is why they are significant points to be considered in the total cost of ownership of the entire process or project.

Another crucial aspect of data to TCO is the pricing data. Ideally, a company utilises separate software designed for cost engineering. This software often contains a separate database of pricing development of raw materials, components and process equipment, which increases the accuracy of quotation calculations, costing activities and forecasts enormously. And even if such software is not available in the company, alternative methods can be applied, such as staying on track of the price development via official forecasts and internal purchasing systems, which contain at least the past data of the pricing. However, the less frequently the purchase of similar kinds of materials, components or equipment happens in the company, the less reliable this data might be for forecasting the future development of the pricing (author's experience). This is the case especially during times of high volatility in the pricing of unique items, such as energy (Eurostat, 2024). In general, the more systematic the follow-up, updating and utilisation of existing price data is, the more accurate it is, as long as done correctly (author's experience).

And so, we arrive at the next port on this fascinating travel across the ocean of TCO, Quality. Sail on!

5   QUALITY AND TCO

In manufacturing, quality is defined as "a measure of excellence or a state of being free from defects, deficiencies and significant variations. It is brought about by strict and consistent commitment to certain standards that achieve uniformity of a product in order to satisfy specific customer or user requirements" (Fowler, 2019). In this chapter, we shall focus on the first three of the four components of quality management:

1. Quality planning
2. Quality assurance
3. Quality control (Hussain, 2023).

The fourth component is quality improvement, but that aspect in TCO shall be covered in Section 5.6, Mutual benefits of Quality and TCO.

5.1   Quality planning and TCO

"Quality planning is a group of strategies that permit you to have a proper outcome from a project." (Indeed Editorial Team, 2023). A quality system consists of the quality plan, quality reports, documentation control and policies, processes, procedures and work instructions. The stakeholders of this planning are the company's own organisation, the customer's organisation, suppliers and other stakeholders (Hermarij, 2021, p. 105), out of which the main drivers come from industry standards, internal requirements and customer requirements (author's own experience). In projects, the quality plan contains the quality expectations and related acceptance criteria (Hermarij, 2021, p. 106), derived from the drivers. With single deliverables, these acceptance criteria are divided into quality criteria, and product descriptions are created. These product descriptions contain:

➢ the quality criteria for verification of each sub-deliverable
➢ the applied quality methods
➢ the skills required to achieve this
➢ the responsibilities of the people included in the process
➢ how to report products outside tolerance.

The quality plan describes interim reviews, verification of meeting the set requirements and validating if the results are usable (Hermarij, 2021, p. 106).

From the TCO perspective, quality planning sets the foundation for all the quality activities in a company. As clear guidelines in general, quality planning makes the entire process of quality management more fluent, reducing rework at every process step. When methods have been defined, communicated and mutually aligned beforehand, all relevant stakeholders will already be aware of the correct methods, required skills and responsibilities. Additionally, when reporting methods and formats have been agreed beforehand with external and internal stakeholders, during a project the reporting and related analysis can be focused on the content of the reports instead of how to report, saving valuable working time and making the whole process more fluent for everyone (author's experience).

5.2 Quality assurance and TCO

"Quality assurance (QA) is any systematic process of determining whether a product or service meets specified requirements. QA establishes and maintains the development or manufacturing of reliable products. The main purpose of a quality assurance system is to increase customer confidence and a company's credibility, improve working processes and efficiency and increase the competitiveness of a company" (Gillis, 2024). This is achieved by reducing the risk of defects and addressing faults as early as possible in the value chain. This is done in practice through both technical and managerial processes. QA system is mainly driven by related ISO standards, mainly ISO 9001, and it is in place to make sure both managerial and technical processes are implemented (ISO, year unknown).

There are basically three QA methods:

➢ failure testing = continuous testing to determine if the product will break or fail

➢ statistical process control (SPC), based on objective data and analysis

➢ total quality management, applying quantitative methods as the basis of continuous improvement (Gillis, 2024).

Just like with the product design, the further upstream in the value chain the defects are spotted and corrected, the more money is saved because of having less failed scope to be corrected. This does not mean these errors and defects cannot still be expensive to resolve, but the further down the value chain these defects are spotted, the more expensive they become in comparison. And if these defects reach the direct customer or end customer, if different from the direct customer, the resulting expenses might become enormous as recall campaigns and negative effect on the reputation of the OEM, and the contract manufacturer, if the manufacturing of one or more products was outsourced (author's experience).

5.3   Quality control and TCO

Quality control (QC) is ensuring a product or service fulfils a predefined set of quality standards and meets the customer requirements. The typical quality control process contains the following steps:

1. setting testing or inspecting standards

2. testing raw materials and various phases of the manufacturing process

3. resolving issues, defining and focusing on the root cause

4. collecting data and making decisions (Indeed Editorial Team, 2024).

In TCO, well-executed QC brings a lot of benefits. Standardised means of testing and inspection bring clarity to how to conduct different tests and inspections, while raw material tests and QC inspections throughout the production process act as checkpoints in tracking down the defects. For example, if a component was checked in the incoming quality control and then in several locations in the production, the easiest starting point is to refer to the QC results in these previous inspection points. This makes the QC process less tedious, consuming fewer working hours and thus it becomes cheaper.

Additionally, when issue resolution is focused on finding and mitigating the root cause of the defect, and preventive measures are put in place to prevent the same defect from reoccurring, the process quality is improved incrementally and reliably, which further saves manufacturing costs. Furthermore, systematic collecting and objective analysis of data together with reported findings creates a solid foundation to make correct decisions concerning the magnitude of countermeasures required to prevent these defects from occurring again. This way, it will be much more likely that the countermeasures won't be insufficient nor overengineered, saving a lot of money in the long run to the entire company (author's experience).

5.4   Risk management and TCO

The ISO 31000 standard defines risk management as a "set of components that provide the foundations and organizational arrangements for designing, implementing, monitoring, reviewing and continually improving risk management processes throughout the organization" (ComplianceOnline, 2024).

Correct identification of the risks early in the project enables the team to plan the preventive actions well, and, if necessary, alternative means of execution of tasks or activities that these risks are related to. A good risk analysis and risk evaluation are the key to the correct prioritization of the risks based on their probability and impact, which will guide the budgeting of funds required to mitigate these risks, especially with risks that require expensive solutions. If there are several "equally good" alternatives for the risk treatment, a TCO analysis can help at choosing the most affordable one (author's experience).

5.5   Cost of poor quality and TCO

Prevention costs are the costs of actions taken to prevent poor quality of products or services. These include, for example, trainings, quality audits, supplier evaluation and process capability studies. Appraisal costs come from the need to hire external consultants or experts to find the causes of poor quality. These can include incoming goods inspection, supplier inspection, laboratory inspection and calibration, for example. On the other hand, the categorisation between internal and external failures is done based on at which point in the value stream the defect was discovered: prior to or after delivering the product to the customer. Internal failures lead to actions like rework, internal scrap, re-testing and rejection costs. External failures lead to things like warranty claims, penalties, recall campaigns and loss of goodwill (Hessing, year unknown). Internal and external failures both contain significant cost elements, but they are not occurring on an "either/or" principle. Whenever a new external failure occurs, one or more of the actions related to internal failure also need to be taken to ensure the same failure won't happen again.

The implementation of the Cost of Poor Quality is a process that contains the following steps:

➢ Definition of organisation's goals and objectives.
➢ Estimation of the capability of current machines, systems and processes.
➢ Collecting data for different cost categories.
➢ Validation of the quality of the cost data together with finance department.
➢ Doing a Pareto analysis of the quality costs.
➢ Implementation of the corrective actions.

> ➢ Comparing the costs of quality before and after the implementation of these process steps. There is typically a modest increase in the cost of good quality that is offset many times over by the savings in the cost of poor quality.
>
> ➢ Presenting the results to the top management (Hessing, year unknown).

Often the costs of poor quality can indeed be easily greater than the costs of good quality. The internal failure costs are calculated as Internal Failure Costs = Costs of Rework + Scrap Costs + Downtime Costs + Other Internal Failure Costs and external failure costs as External Failure Costs = Warranty Costs + Customer Returns + Product Recall Costs + Other External Failure Costs (SSDSI, 2023). Let's bring up an example: due to the complexity of the product, the scrap rate on one process station has been 15% of the products, even though the operator working on the station is known to be committed and knowledgeable in quality inspections. This has made the process engineer wonder if something should be done about the station itself. It turns out the company missed a customer requirement of having a QC camera system in place during the planning and execution phase of setting up the new production process, and this customer requirement was based on the customer's own experience. Even though the Total Cost of Ownership for the camera system is 400 000 €, process engineer still calculates the comparison of the costs of good quality and cost of poor quality, knowing the production will still be running for four years after the delivery, installation and commissioning of the camera system. Since the appraisal costs have been running since the discovery of this defect and will be running until the QC camera system is in place, this will be equal in both cases, thus not affecting the calculation. The total manufacturing value of the product at the point of next quality check and outlet is 500 € and the production volume remaining after camera system implementation will be 80 000 units. With this calculation, we get already as a direct cost of poor quality 15% x 500 €/unit x 80 000 units = 6 000 000 €, meaning 1,5 million € per year, giving a payback period of 3,2 months. And this doesn't even include the overtime required to catch up with the required production volumes, expenses from continuous appraisals over 4 years and so on.

5.6   Mutual benefits of Quality and TCO

As shown in the imaginary example in the previous section, it is very useful to compare the TCO of good quality and TCO of poor quality. After all, especially in the tight financial situation, the management might very easily stop investing in anything else than what is necessary. On the other hand, there might be a temptation to skip the quality improvements that are not necessarily required to achieve the set quality targets. However, there are multiple situations in which it is still easily cheaper to invest in quality improvements than not to. And in the most extreme cases, in which the entire production process has been ramped up focusing only on quantity, skipping quality altogether, the result might very well be a grim financial situation for the entire company.

For example, modification of one production cell during a project in which the entire production line is modified, would cost 100 000 € in initial purchase costs because of synergies with the rest of the project, while the modification done afterwards would cost 160 000 €. The management is inclined to refuse any unnecessary modifications outside the scope of the project but requests a payback period calculation anyway. With the help of the process quality team and the technical expert of the equipment being modified, the cost engineer defines that maintenance costs of the equipment would remain unaltered, same for the process utilities. However, the rework time would be reduced by 45 seconds per product on average, and scrap costs reduced by 10 000 € per year. The production will run for 3 years with an annual volume of 10 000 units per year. The required training costs for the operators to operate the new equipment are 10 000 € in total and this process improvement would not affect the automation rate of this station. The wage costs of the rework station operators are 28 €/h per person. However, whether the number of operators can be reduced or not depends on the total workload reduction. Additionally, the process utilities and consumables for the rework station cost 2 €/h, which is constant per rework hour.

Obviously, doing this change during the project would be cheaper overall. Thus, we get the comparison of 100 000 € versus the cost of poor quality, which is calculated:

➢ Rework time in total = 45 seconds per product x 10 000 units per year x 3 years / 3600 seconds per hour = 375 hours in total.

➢ Thus, the utility and consumable costs are 750 €.

➢ Operator unit wage costs won't be considered because this time saving won't allow the reduction of the number of operators even with rebalancing of the production.

➢ Scrap costs for the total period of 3 years are 30 000 €.

➢ In total these two are 30 750 €.

Based on this calculation, the top management decides to refuse from investing in this process improvement. But soon the top management gets contacted by the customer, with a claim of 60% of the total warranty costs of the previous model of the product based on the issue caused by the poor quality in this exact process phase. These costs total up at 280 000 € and include a demand to fix this issue immediately. And this way, the top management has no choice but to approve of this process improvement.

If quoting children's stories at this point, the "moral of the story" is that besides the direct and indirect costs, also financial risks must be included in the equation in financial decision making. And if this issue has been included in the risk register of the project, the chances are this risk was known already and possibly the mitigation measures have already been planned. After all, financial risks are a part of TCO.

Aside from this, TCO can also benefit quality improvements in multiple other ways than calculations. One of the most important benefits of successful TCO work for quality improvements is the improved profitability of the company, which gives the company "financial breathing space" to afford the required process improvements. And when Total Cost of Ownership and Cost of Quality are combined, the true cost of good quality compared to cost of poor quality can be estimated much more accurately, and as in general with TCO, it guides the thinking of the stakeholders towards all the related cost items, included trying to figure out all the related hidden costs. All in all, the good quality creates a positive cycle in TCO:

1) Quality improvements help reduce rework and scrap
2) resulting in improved productivity and throughput
3) which in turn improves profitability
4) which might allow for more funds to plan and execute further quality improvements, starting a new cycle.

6 STRATEGY AND TCO

After quality, we get to the next aspect of TCO, strategy. Even though there is relatively little available in the literature concerning the connection between the two, they go hand in hand. And because there is very little available in literature about the connection between TCO and strategy, it is good to approach this topic from an additional viewpoint: healthy corporate finance and strategy. After all, the good financial status of the company allows making the investments and other purchases required to achieve the set strategic goals and to explore different strategies more bravely, while the company strategy guides the TCO work by highlighting the key focus areas of the company. If the TCO work within a company remains disconnected from the strategy and core businesses, a lot of the huge value-adding potential of Total Cost of Ownership is lost (author's own experience).

6.1 How is TCO tied to strategy?

The strategy of an organisation describes how it is going to bring value to its owners, customers and citizens. For example, if over 75% of a company's value is formed by intangible capital, developing intangible capital should be the focus of the creation and execution of the strategy (Kaplan & Norton, 2004, p. 27). Usually, a lot of the capital of a manufacturing industry company is tangible, but this doesn't mean the TCO work must or should be limited only to that. As we shall discuss further in Chapter 8, we humans are the ones running the companies, working in them and operating the tangible assets.

The company's strategy begins with understanding the strategic position of the company. And one of the tools to analyse the macro-level strategic position is the PESTEL analysis, which highlights six macro-environment aspects:

- political

- economic

- social

- technological

- ecological

- legal (Whittington et al., 2020, p. 36).

And even though the economic factor is one of the six in the PESTEL analysis, all six affect the TCO of the entire company and its operations. From a political point of view, the role of the state and potential pressure from civil society organisations can both affect what kind of options can be considered viable in decision-making in business, potentially removing the options with the lowest TCO. In the economic factor, things such as currency exchange rates, interest rates and economic up- and downturns affect the strategic position of a company. Understanding the trends in these areas helps to lower the TCO, for example, by reducing overall funding costs and enabling the choosing of the more favourable currency when doing business with companies from the regions with different currencies. From the social perspective, innovation, power and effectiveness, and economic growth rate in general are shaped by demographics, distribution of wealth, geography and culture. For example, there can be major differences in facility cost levels and pay levels in different areas within one country, which can be leveraged for added profit if the increased logistics costs won't offset this saving. In the technological aspect, many organisations publish technology roadmaps illustrating the future of their field of business, forecasting the timeline for the adoption of these technologies and the timeline for the need of related goods and services required to implement these technologies. And this helps in the planning of related activities within these companies. New technologies also sometimes make it possible to manufacture the goods at lower costs.

The ecological viewpoint focuses on macro-environmental topics such as pollution, waste and climate change. Environmental regulation both creates additional costs and presents new business opportunities for companies, for example in recycling and pollution reduction. The legal aspect is also important to understand, because it contains a lot of cost elements such as minimum wages, overtime fees, working time regulation, taxation and so on (Whittington et al., 2020, pp. 36-47).

Aside from the macro-level strategy, there are other strategy topics that have a lot to do with the total cost of ownership. For example, reliable financial calculations are required to support the product strategy; if a company is planning to try to obtain new customers from its competitors with the differentiation of its products, the management needs to know how much is the forecasted additional revenue that might be gained with the differentiation and how much additional costs is created in the process. In doing a full TCO analysis of this differentiation, the management will have a reliable financial decision-making basis if the forecasted added revenue ends up being close to reality, or better yet, if the actualised revenue ends up exceeding the initial forecast. Another aspect of the strategy is the manufacturing capacity: How big is the annual sales volume forecast? Are there big fluctuations in it from one year to another? Are there any major or mega trends affecting the demand positively or negatively right now or in sight in the near future? All these questions and more will have an impact on the production volume targets and, for example, the in-house manufacturing rate, meaning how big a share of the manufacturing could be outsourced. And all these questions affect also the total cost of ownership of the complete production process. In contract manufacturing, these production volumes often come from the customer organisation. Depending on the structure and maturity of the customer organisation, the contract manufacturer may also propose alternative production volume scenarios (author's experience).

6.2   Higher CAPEX or OPEX?

As long as the production process is not over-engineered, in the manufacturing process and related immediate support functions, the ratio between CAPEX and OPEX can be looked upon as in inverse proportion. This means that when one goes up, the other one goes down. After all, it is not physically possible to exceed the operating speeds of the existing technology or "operating speeds" of us humans. However, this is not always the case with other functions, such as production control, facility or finance, which is why in this section we focus on the context of the manufacturing process, and more strictly the choice between higher CAPEX or higher OPEX. However, the choice between higher CAPEX or higher OPEX is still a strategic one, which means we shall discuss this aspect here in this section, leaving manufacturing process specific TCO topics to Chapter 10.

The financial situation forms one cornerstone of the strategic planning in a company, because different strategies often require different amounts of monetary resources at different timelines. And here TCO is an irreplaceable tool if applied correctly: As discussed e.g. in the section 3.4, TCO improves the accuracy of financial estimates both in the sums of money and timing, because together with a good technical understanding it is possible to include a huge variety of hidden costs in the equation, which will improve the reliability of the financial calculations required for the funding discussions. And this funding might be necessary to afford the CAPEX investments planned to achieve the strategic goals. Understanding the funding, its sources and the timing when the funds will be available is also crucial to the choice between higher CAPEX or OPEX when planning and building up a manufacturing process. But there are also cases where the choices of higher CAPEX and higher OPEX are not equal in viability. For example, in certain countries if a company wishes to outsource parts of or the full manufacturing of one or more of its products, it will favour higher OPEX or even 100% OPEX from the manufacturing process through unit price due to bureaucratical challenges related to state ownership or funding by the state (author's experience). On the other hand, some technological solutions don't allow manual operations, but require an expensive piece of machinery instead. In both cases, the manufacturer needs to investigate the needs of funding and seek it from different potential sources, which could be, for example, retained earnings, debt capital and equity capital (Investopedia, 2024).

In business-to-business trading between OEM and contract manufacturer the payment criteria may also be related to the CAPEX investments of the manufacturer, and on the other hand the OEM customer may want to try to shift as big a proportion of the payment to unit price instead of lump sums during the production process build up to shift away the financial risk towards the contract manufacturer (author's experience).

6.3   What does the customer need?

Even though the old saying goes, "The customer is always right", sometimes the customer doesn't know what he or she needs. There might be many reasons for this, for example, having analysed the market wrongly, leading to over-optimistic or over-pessimistic sales forecasts, or not knowing all the suitable technological solutions available to manufacture the product. Besides the lack of knowledge and incorrect forecasts, the simple lack of funds may limit the choices the customer might have. In the case of a startup company, especially if the product is not very high-end, it might be wise to start with a lower automation rate and lower production volumes, if there are not "tons" of preorders already available. Both choices lead to lower investment needs during the production process build-up, and lower related OPEX costs. However, when retaining the production volumes at the planned level, the lower automation rate directly leads to an increased amount of manual labour, which means increased OPEX costs.

Another aspect of what the customer needs is the targeted market areas of the product. In the context of strategy, the selection of targeted market areas is ultimately based on the forecasts of related revenue versus related costs. In other words, whether expanding to further market areas would bring in additional profit or not (author's own experience).

6.4 Mutual benefits between strategy and TCO

There's an enormous variety of benefits shared mutually between strategy work and TCO work, due to which it is surprising how little research there is on this topic. Improved accuracy of forecasts related to financial scenarios in strategy work, having a solid financial foundation for good organisational agility and resilience and having the financial "freedom" to execute the planned strategy are some of the key benefits that successful TCO work can bring to the company through improved accuracy of different forecasts and overall improved profitability, if this improved profitability isn't all used to fill the pockets of the company's owners.

On the other hand, having a realistic and well-communicated strategy with clear and concrete goals and related activities and actions is very important for the success of TCO to utilize the full benefits from it by aiming the efforts of TCO effectively to there where they make the biggest difference with the allocated effort. Not only that, but since the top management is usually responsible for the company's strategy, bringing TCO and strategy together gives top management clarity to TCO work and very likely increasing the level of management commitment to TCO work within the company. And achieving management commitment is necessary to gain commitment from the rest of the organisation (GrowEQ, 2023).

7   STAKEHOLDERS AND TCO

So far in this book, we have mostly considered the operations within a company with a few references to business between customer and supplier. However, as the whole concept is about a comprehensive view of costs, we also must consider other stakeholders than single teams or single functions within a company. Both cost effects and mutual benefits of cross-functional collaboration within a company and between the company and external stakeholders must be considered, too.

7.1   Internal stakeholders and TCO

When aiming to improve the company's performance through Total Cost of Ownership, understanding who are the internal stakeholders of our decision-making, and how they are affected by our decisions must be one of our top priorities. After all, trying to improve the company profitability by isolated savings in separate functions and teams would be like trying to clean up our yard in the Autumn by blowing all the fallen leaves to the neighbour's side and getting some new leaves to our yard from surrounding trees afterwards. This just leads to a seemingly effective method to save time, which eventually results in a situation in which nobody gained anything and now there's more work for everyone to do to clear the leaves. Another example: especially in big companies, every decision, no matter how small it might seem, has multiple internal stakeholders. For example, whether we get twenty or forty sets of test parts now, and the rest later, will decide whether all the commissioning tests of the process equipment can be done, including all the required tests. This is why it is important to know the functions of the company, and their purposes and main activities, because without this understanding we do not have a solid decision-making basis to reduce the costs throughout the whole value stream, end to end, opposite to organisational silos, which we shall cover in the section 8.10. When needing to prioritize between the stakeholders, both internal and external, we can resort to stakeholder mapping. In this book, different internal functions are discussed in the context of TCO in Chapter 12.

Employees are also one group of stakeholders, especially when it comes to decisions made by the top management. After all, our income as employees often at least mostly or even 100% depends on the salary income. We also form perhaps the most important production factor. In addition, we expect to hold a stake in the company, the expression from which the term "stakeholder" comes. In the common expectation, this is the case especially for the direct employees of the company (Crane et al., 2019, p. 287-290). More about employees and TCO, however, in the chapter Human aspect and TCO.

7.2 External stakeholders and TCO

And now we come to the main point of this chapter: external stakeholders. After all, a company is dependent on its customers, owners and suppliers and, in many cases, also on the financial community. On the other hand, a company is also affected by the state and civil society, and the company affects local communities and consumers outside the company's customer segment in general. And this is also important to understand when looking for TCO saving potentials. Onwards with the words of the old, highly "worn" saying "customer first".

7.2.1 Customers

"*Revenue is the money generated from normal business operations, calculated as the average sales price times the number of units sold. It is the top line (or gross income) figure from which costs are subtracted to determine net income. Revenue is also known as sales on the income statement.*" (Hayes, 2024). In practice, this means the primary source of income in business comes from sales to a customer or, in most cases, to multiple customers. And this is why I think it is crucial to consider how a customer might be affected by the internal TCO work and how the customer can see the "TCO in action" directly.

The first time when a potential customer gets to look at what results from a well understood Total Cost of Ownership of the goods and services being offered is the binding quotation for the whole work scope, unless there is a separate phase of a price indication preceding the binding quotation, which often is the case in the deals worth millions made between major companies. If the potential supplier understands well the whole TCO of what is being quoted, this should be apparent in the cost breakdown of the quotation, given the potential supplier is willing to give out this detailed breakdown. This in turn helps the potential customer company to understand what it would be paying for, where the cost-saving potentials could be found and if the pricing level is reasonable (4cost, 2008–2024). This also gives the customer confidence that the supplier knows what it is doing, both through the professional look of the quotation and good technical understanding of the scope of work being quoted for. Additionally, when the potential supplier understands the whole TCO of the work scope well, there usually are fewer negative surprises in the means of costs coming either to the way of the customer or the way of the supplier (author's experience). Of course, TCO alone is not some "miraculous medicine that cures all the price fluctuations and force majeure cases" but by applying it and paying attention to all the hidden costs, the chances of sudden negative surprises in costs are much lower (author's experience). In general, the buyer can utilize the TCO analysis to evaluate the alternative quotations from supplier candidates and to drive the process improvement while the seller can utilize TCO models to measure, document and communicate the added value the seller's proposal brings to the buyer compared to the competing quotations (Piscopo et al., 2008).

Additionally, major quotations often contain a lot of negotiating between the two parties after submitting the binding quotation until signing the agreement. During these negotiations, a good understanding of the TCO of the work scope is vital in guiding the work to find true cost-saving potentials. By "digging out" the hidden costs that neither negotiation party would have understood without putting their minds to it, it becomes clearer which proposed cost-saving solution would save costs and which one would not. And in the ideal case this work carries on throughout the planning and execution of the work after signing the agreement, both discovering saving potentials and ideally sharing them between the two parties and, when conditions change or something was forgotten in the quotation phase, bringing these unforeseen costs to the light early on. Of course, this can be one point of the contract negotiations: In case the saving potentials are found or additional costs incurred, how are they shared between the two parties?

7.2.2 Owners

Business owners create the company's vision, mission and long-term objectives and establish the strategic direction, as well as support the top management at achieving these goals. The business owners are also big influencers at establishing and maintaining the culture of a company (MBB Management, 2023). And this description is more typical to those business owners who work actively in the company. However, there is also another type of owner group, shareholders. Their support is usually more of the financial type, providing financial security through the shares they have purchased. And these shares in turn give the shareholders a right to receive dividends when they are paid and have a voting power in certain situations (Your company formations, 2024). For the latter group, shareholders, the company share value is the key driver. Some company-specific factors affecting the pricing of the shares are:

- news releases on earnings and profits and estimates of future earnings

- announcements of dividends

- introduction of a new product

- product recalls

- securing a large new contract

- employee layoffs

- anticipated takeover or merger

- a change in management

- accounting errors or scandals (Ontario Securities Commission, 2024).

Out of these, the ones that benefit the most from TCO work are current and estimated future earnings and profits, ability to pay dividends, as well as the chances to secure a large new contract. Sometimes the "detective work" required by the TCO modelling can also uncover potential risks of recall indirectly, because TCO requires cross-functional collaboration, thanks to which it is possible to spot these risks more effectively (author's experience). Many of these benefits are related to the points explained in Chapters 3 and 6, as well as Section 2.5.

7.2.3 Suppliers

In this section, we focus on how the suppliers of a manufacturing company are affected by TCO. The explanation is done at general level, because some details of supply chain management and TCO are explained in Chapter 11. Additionally, the points that were already explained in Section 7.2.1 do also apply here; it is just a matter of reversed roles by the contract manufacturer, for example, acting now as a buyer, not as a seller. Aside from the previously made points, the collaboration between the contract manufacturer and its suppliers can benefit from TCO enormously. This is a question of internal cross-functional collaboration, which brings added value to the collaboration between the buyer and the seller. These aspects include, for example:
- enhanced understanding of the cost breakdown
- improved predictability of the pricing and how it is proportionate to production volumes
  - this reduces pressure on both sides, if the buyer has managed to secure a reasonable budget for the supplier equipment and parts through TCO work
- improved understanding of the internal costs related to the supplier

- the finances of both buyer and seller benefit from TCO combined with win-win negotiation targets (author's experience).

At this point, I would like to explain the improved understanding of the internal costs related to the supplier a bit further, taking the case of outsourcing parts of a product as an example. For a supplier to manufacture the parts of a product that its customer wants to outsource, it needs certain data items, such as drawings including tolerances, product data and other technical documentation, such as relevant industry and customer-specific standards and norms. If there are no simple instructions nor competence available about how to arrange these to the supplier, the resulting documentation can be of very poor quality, which leads to big amounts of rework and even expensive mistakes in the process. The bigger the internal team in the contract manufacturer's organisation doing this work, the more the piled-up amount of rework might cost in money. Which is why in contexts like this I always like to advise: Let's first look into the mirror and think what we did wrong instead of hindering fluent supplier relations.

7.2.4 Local community

This is one aspect that is often forgotten in the decision-making process outside those topics that require considering this stakeholder group, too. The local community is also affected by successful TCO work, especially if we are talking about a small town with only one or two major companies and several smaller businesses. One of the most immediate effects is that successful TCO work at the local major manufacturer's organisation improves the profitability of the company, leading to less pressure to lay people off in an economic downturn and more chances to hire people and grow sustainably.

On the other hand, the full TCO analyses carried out by these major companies might prove that some services or goods previously sourced from other towns or even abroad can be procured cheaper overall from the local suppliers due to the benefits of synergy, short distances and very quick reaction times in case of sudden changes in when and how many components or assemblies are required to run the production. This brings added work to these smaller local enterprises, often leading to chances to grow the business and hire more people. This creates a positive cycle, because more work locally means more funds acquired by the town or city through taxation to improve the local services and facilities, which leads to higher standards of living for the locals. And this might make it lucrative for more people to move in, which feeds this positive cycle even further (author's experience).

7.2.5 State and civil society

Next, we shift our focus from the local community to the wider national spectrum affecting the laws and political pressures: state and civil society. After all, it is the state, sometimes directed by a higher regional political power, such as the European Union, that brings in new laws and changes to existing ones, possibly affecting the macro-environment in business.

One of the most direct effects on companies coming from the state and the regional political and legal institutions is the legislation affecting the region or country in which the company operates. This is the case for both multinationals and companies residing in a single country. To understand what external "forces" affect TCO work in the company, one way is to turn to the political and legal aspects of PESTEL analysis, shortly introduced in Chapter 6. For example, customs and tariffs have an effect in three ways:

- They affect the total cost of ownership of a purchase within the same economic area compared to a purchase of goods or services produced in a different economic area.
- They affect the negotiations in some cases: what delivery terms buyer and seller prefer?
- The related paperwork and other tasks often require quite a workload from one person or a team, depending on the size of the company and volume of the goods being purchased from abroad.

Laws and changes in them might also affect the TCO work. If a favourable or unfavourable change in law is coming up, it might be wise to proceed, for example, with an enormous investment soon before an unfavourable change in law is applied. Another aspect of the state and civil society and their effect on total cost of ownership of a complete business or its functions is the wage cost. This differs greatly from one country to another, but in many countries, there are vacation fees, overtime extra pays, minimum salaries and so on. This affects the unit wage cost of the workforce. But legislation can also affect this cost through fringe benefits and incidental wage expenses, which are paid by the company on top of the employee's salary. And in many countries these wage levels are affected by two-way negotiations between employers' and employees' unions or three-way negotiations, in which case also the government is involved in the negotiation. For example, in Germany the effect of the labour union is very strong in wage levels and plans to close factories or reduce workforce (author's experience).

7.2.6 Consumers

This section is very short, but that does not diminish its meaningfulness one bit. But this is one of those parts where this book differs from a 100% schoolbook. After all, one of the intrinsic motivations for me to write about TCO has been to spread the knowledge of an alternative method of saving costs in business, rather than the traditional cost-cutting efforts.

Through the successful TCO work and the lowered total costs in result the companies can keep the prices competitive and even lower them below market averages, bringing added value directly to their customers who buy the product, and indirectly by creating pressure for competitors to find means to reach the same cost levels while retaining the similar levels of functionality. That is, if the cost savings are not just pocketed by the business owners throughout the industry. Personally, I want to emphasize that the same pie being shared by more people brings benefit to everyone in the long run. The increased purchasing power of us consumers will encourage us to consume, which will increase the sales volumes, offsetting the unit price reduction in many cases by a big enough margin to increase the total revenue (author's view).

7.2.7 Banks and creditors

To finish this chapter, we discuss the banks and creditors, the one from whom a business can seek additional funds required to achieve its strategic goals. Many of these benefits of TCO in this context are described also elsewhere within this book, but let's gather them up under this title to bring the focus here, in case someone someday would hopefully get to utilize this knowledge.

Successful TCO work benefits both banks and creditors and the company itself in several ways. Since loans pretty much always come with an interest rate, it is favourable to avoid unnecessary loans. Even though TCO alone doesn't guarantee a company will never need to apply for a loan, it can guide the financial forecasts related to the quotation calculations both in the sums of money and timing closer to the finally actualising figures. These forecasts are used as the negotiation basis when negotiating payment steps and payment criteria with the customer. In case the investments required to complete a project are paid by the customer "over the table" throughout the project, for example, the correctness of the initial estimate is important to preserve the liquidity of the project, meaning the required purchases would be done using the funds from customer payments. If there is only one major project in the whole company going on, binding most of the workforce to it, the liquidity of the project might very easily correlate with the liquidity of the whole company during this project, if there are no simultaneous sources of revenue. However, a company may also need to secure other sources of funding.

Another benefit of the improved accuracy of financial forecasts is the lowered risk of suddenly needing a major loan or, alternatively, canceling other planned investments required to execute the chosen strategy. This provides a stable decision-making basis for the top management, often contributing to the overall success of the company. Additionally, the data from these forecasts is also used in loan applications, because funders also require information about when and how much money is needed and when and in how big sums it can be paid back. The improved accuracy of forecasts thus increases the confidence of banks and other creditors (author's experience). These all together with the improved financial performance of a business also benefit the credit rating of a company (Kagan, 2024). And the credit rating tells the banks and other creditors how high the risk is that the borrower might struggle to pay its debts back in the future. A low credit rating might limit the amount of funds available to be loaned and increase the interest rate charged for the loan (Alternative Business Funding, 2024).

8 HUMAN ASPECT AND TCO

And so, our TCO ship arrives at the last port on this leg of our journey: The human aspect. As I have already mentioned previously in the book, the human aspect is my primary motivation to write this whole book. After all, it's us humans who form the working organisations, and many of us don't have other simultaneous sources of income aside from the salary we get from work. But not to worry, dear Reader, despite this being my motivation to write this complete book, I shall not "resort" to idealism in this chapter, skipping the research on the matter. That would not be very convincing, would it?

In this chapter we shall focus on organisational behaviour, humanity and leadership in TCO. Basically, this chapter together with Chapter 4 forms the core of TCO optimisation of teamwork in a project. On top of that, we shall also investigate topics very rarely, if ever, discussed in TCO:

- Layoffs and big recruitment campaigns
- High performing teams
- The currently trending topic of remote/office/hybrid
- Organisational silos and lazy thinking

And what do these topics have to do with the TCO? A lot, as we shall discover. Let's start with us human beings as the foundation for TCO success, because we are not mere "expenses in the balance sheet"; we are living and breathing and productive creatures.

8.1 Humans as a foundation for TCO success

Deep down, planning and implementing TCO work in an organisation is "like any big change in the ways of working". This means it requires good leadership of the change. Change leadership is a field of study that I highly recommend getting to know to be successful at implementing a TCO change, but we shall not include much of it in the scope of this book. In this section we shall focus on humans and TCO in the context of people working in an organisation.

We humans are not only crucial for the successful implementation of TCO in a working organisation and incorporating it into our daily work, but we also are a part of the Total Cost of Ownership of running a business. Fluent collaboration and information exchange, our motivation and engagement to work, the mutual respect and communication within the team; these affect the TCO of our teamwork. And on top of intrinsic motivations, our motivation and engagement can be affected by external factors, such as whether the tools we need for our work are usable, useful and understandable, and if the design of the things and equipment we need to operate to do our job is good or not. The negative TCO effects of these things include:

- extended training periods
- decreased engagement to work, leading to reduced work output, which in turn leads to the need of additional recruitments
- user frustration, which can reduce job engagement, potentially leading to additional recruitment needs
- different errors caused by poor design leading to accumulation of rework and issue resolution costs
- all above potentially to vacant jobs in the company taking longer to fill
- all above together hindering the company from achieving its strategic objectives and goals.

Eventually, the low-cost solution becomes a high-cost solution and ending up in a quiet failure and all the money and effort being wasted. For example, one software case showed that Human Total Cost of Ownership, HTCO, of training and retraining to replace those who dropped out of the training program, was around $110,000 per employee. And that did not include the additional cost to the company caused by user errors and the administrative work to cope with these errors because of the software being user-hostile. This additional cost was another $115,000, bringing the total HTCO cost resulting from the wrong choice of software to $225,000 per employee (Hoffman et al., 2008, p 203). Let's multiply this by 10 employees, for example, and we get $2,250,000, or roughly 2,08 million € (xe currency converter, 2024). Let's say the user-friendly software would have cost an additional 10 000 € per license annually, including the maintenance fee, and the software is needed for five years for ten people. Choosing the user-friendly option would have thus cost 500 000 € more to purchase and maintain than the user-hostile option. However, if we assume that the share between training and retraining cost of $110 000 was roughly 50/50, we could in the best case save roughly 1,07 million € by choosing the user-friendly option.

8.2   Organisational hierarchy of needs & TCO

We people have needs, goals and aspirations, for example achieving the expertise that our jobs require and expanding the range of our expertise. We also prefer working in an environment that is what we need to perform our assignments in a satisfying and gratifying manner. Meeting these needs is also very important to achieving the strategic goals of an organisation (Hoffman et al., 2008, p. 202).

Another way to put this is by applying Maslow's hierarchy of needs, probably the best-known early motivation theory, to working organisations. This model contains a pyramid, in that the next layer builds up on top of the previous one:

1. Physiological needs

2. Safety-security needs

3. Social-belongingness needs

4. Esteem needs

5. Self-actualisation needs

6. (Intrinsic values). This one has been introduced quite recently but hasn't yet gained widespread acceptance (Robbins & Judge, 2022, p. 130).

The five original groups of needs can also be applied in the working environment. On the first level, employees need, for example, access to fresh drinking water and restrooms, a chance to eat during the workday and a comfortable working environment. On the second level, we people need to feel that we and our belonging are safe and protected, including our physical health, including good working ergonomics. Another aspect of the need for safety is emotional safety, for example, being able to trust in the continuity of the work. The third level at work is about belonging. If we don't feel a sense of belonging at work, it might affect our motivation and engagement negatively. Establishing and forming relationships at work, which promotes the feeling of belonging, can be supported by the employer, for example, by hosting social events and providing more opportunities for team-building outside the office. This tends to lead to reduced personnel turnover and enhanced job engagement.

Fourth level, esteem, means the feeling of contributing towards a higher goal and that these contributions bring us recognition. This means feeling of growth, advancement and achievement. When we are confident of ourselves and our abilities and we receive positive feedback and support, we are more likely to succeed. And if the feedback only comes during the annual review, this may affect the employee esteem negatively. The final level, self-actualisation, means at work that we have the intrinsic need to feel we are doing the best we can at work, which motivates us to continue on our career path and succeed. This means we need opportunities in which we can feel this. To feel self-actualised at work, we need challenges that are not overwhelming nor overloading, but not too easy as well. Employers, or the direct supervisors in bigger companies, can also help employees feel self-actualised by helping them look for ways of career advancement in well-fit roles (Herrity, 2024).

When these needs are met, we are more productive, engaged and creative at work, which also improves the quality of our work, resulting in better solutions that can even increase the revenue of the company and reduce the cost of rework when the quality of our work is improved (author's experience).

8.3   Human leadership and TCO

From the organisational hierarchy of needs, we shift to leadership. After all, how we are led affects many components of our performance at work. Leadership, leading others and being led is never a simple business, especially since we all are individuals, and different things motivate us, make us push harder and drive us forward (author's experience). However, in this section we shall focus on the leadership traits that are generally in the study of leadership considered as desirable or undesirable and their effects on Total Cost of Ownership of running a business.

What then makes a good leader? According to Rebecca Knight in her writing on the Harvard Business Review blog, the 8 qualities of a successful leader are:

1. authenticity to who you are
2. curiosity about things "outside the box"
3. analytical prowess and understanding of cause-and-effect relationships
4. adaptability in the face of change
5. fostering a workplace culture that supports creativity
6. comfort with ambiguity of competing ideas and competing priorities
7. resilience in the face of a challenge or failure
8. empathy and emotional intelligence (Knight, 2023).

And how do these affect the HTCO? Authenticity leads to people having faith in their leaders and being satisfied with them. Authenticity also empowers people (Robbins & Judge, 2022, p. 231). Curiosity helps the leader look at the organisation from "outside-in", seeing the situations and issues from an external stakeholder's perspective. This helps the leader make more informed decisions thanks to considering the broader context (Knight, 2023). Analytical prowess is a great asset in problem solving, because finding the true root causes of issues and resolving them requires an analytical mindset instead of assuming a typical cause. In engineering work, for example, issue resolution is a part of daily work, and when the leader shows an example of analytical prowess, it spreads in the organisation (author's experience). With analytical prowess come analytical techniques of breaking complex issues down into more understandable elements, making it easier to find the genuine problems and come up with solutions to them (Hermarij, 2021, pp. 494-499).

Adaptability fosters an agile team culture (Knight, 2023). And agile organisations can respond to strategic opportunities and threats relatively fast and easily, as well as detect coming environmental shifts and can act on them as they emerge. (Whittington et al., 2020, p. 454). We people are prepared to change, but not against our own will. And this is an important note when trying to mitigate change resistance: When we are allowed our say and, better yet, have our influence on our own future, we are less likely to resist the change (Hermarij, 2021, pp. 255-256). Fostering a creative atmosphere can bring enormous value to the company. After all, creativity is one of the key drivers of innovation. However, creativity doesn't come from just telling the team to be creative. Desire to work on something because it's challenging, interesting, exciting, and satisfying correlates strongly with creative outputs. As we shall discuss further in Section 8.5, organisational behaviour can also be guided through rewarding and recognition, and to guide the behaviour towards creativity, it needs to be incorporated in the incentive criteria. Additionally, having excessive rules must be discouraged when trying to facilitate creativity, because over-engineering rules restricts creativity (Robbins & Judge, 2022, pp. 125-127).

Being able to handle ambiguity helps at understanding how things are connected and enables considering opposite ideas in the face of uncertainty, managing to avoid overlooking the interdependencies of different dynamics, for example (Knight, 2023), leading to better decision-making (author's experience). Resilience refers to an organisation's capacity to recover from shocks relatively fast and easily, and it is crucial in turbulent environments (Whittington et al., 2020, p. 454), for example in the automotive industry during these times of economic downturn and the failure of battery electric vehicles to meet the enormous sales expectations (author's experience). Empathy and emotional intelligence are important for actively engaging with team members and building relationships and trust. Empathy refers to the ability to "step into other people's shoes", meaning seeing things from their point of view and understanding their priorities (Knight, 2023). Emotional intelligence refers to a person's ability to distinguish emotions in oneself and others, understand the meaning of these emotions and regulate own emotions accordingly. This helps leaders to stay calm under pressure, to solve issues and conflicts more effectively and to be more empathetic with team members and colleagues (Robbins & Judge, 2022, p. 84).

Based on the research on the topic, these traits cover a big share of those widely considered to be the signs of a good leader. What then, makes a terrible leader? This can be just as subjective as what kind of leader is considered good. And to make this topic even more complex, there is no one cross-culturally universal answer to this. To be a good leader in an environment different environment from one is used to, the leader is often pushed to adapt to the cultural reality he or she is facing (Browaeys & Price, 2019, p. 225). But to answer the question, let's do an example. Again, this perception is not the same everywhere in the world, but here in Finland this applies very much: the resentment against being micromanaged. To many of us, self-determination is important, which means our well-being and performance are affected by our motivation for the job activities. This motivation is driven by the feeling of having the choice of what methods we apply to perform the required tasks and having a choice what we do, how motivating the task itself is, how incentives guide this motivation, and how the work satisfies our psychological needs (Robbins & Judge, 2022, p. 133). And when being constantly micromanaged, taking away our liberty to choose the means of the execution of our work within the limits of company rules and available tools, we can also lose our motivation. I have personally experienced this sometimes, and if you, dear reader, haven't, I sincerely hope you never will.

How is this all then related to TCO? All these aspects affect the performance of a working organisation, affecting its productivity, creativity and the quality of its work, which leads to either decreased or increased costs for the same output of results (author's experience).

8.4   Job engagement and TCO

Commitment is a powerful word. The Merriam-Webster dictionary describes commitment as "an agreement or pledge to do something in the future" (Merriam-Webster, 2024). In this context, both managerial and employee commitment are equally important. However, as already pointed out earlier in this book, for example, the Chapter 5, the commitment by top management is of utmost importance to achieving anything.

In this section of the book, we can call organisational commitment also the job engagement of the personnel. Employee engagement means "the degree of enthusiasm an employee feels for the job". Highly engaged employees have a shared passion for the job and feel a deep connection to their employing companies, while disengaged employees put their time, but not their energy nor focus, on the work. The major benefits of high-average employee engagement levels are:

- high levels of customer satisfaction
- improved productivity
- higher profitability
- decreased personnel turnover rate
- reduced proneness to accidents (Robbins & Judge, 2022, p. 67).

All these together form an enormous cost-saving potential. Which is why I claim that succeeding at facilitating and fostering a workplace culture in which everyone can feel and does feel engaged in their work is a true win-win for everyone in the company (author's view).

How can the engagement be promoted, then? Through employee involvement, for example. Employee involvement and participation is a process in which the input comes from employees when they are allowed to participate in decision-making to increase their commitment to the organisational success. And this is done through participative management, which can increase the productivity and morale of an organisation, as well as reduce the negative effect of job insecurity on job satisfaction. And these effects are not typical only to the individuals presented with the opportunity to join in decision-making. Same effects occur in whole teams when they're given more control over their work (Robbins & Judge, 2022, p. 155).

8.5   Wage & rewarding and TCO

As already pointed out earlier in this book, for example in Chapter 2, incentives guide the organisational behaviour. This also applies to promoting the ways of working to achieve the lowest overall Total Cost of Ownership. The personnel wage costs are also a part of the TCO of running a business. Both aspects are discussed in this section.

Even though pay is not the only motivator at work, and perhaps not as strong a motivator as the work-life fit and enjoying the work, it does motivate people. According to Robbins & Judge, a survey conducted by the American Psychological Association indicated that approximately 60% of respondents were staying in their current work because of the pay and benefits. The pay contains two aspects of equity: internal equity, the worth of the job to the organisation, and external equity, "the competitiveness of an organisation's pay relative to pay in its industry". An ideal pay system shows what the job is worth as well as if the salary remains competitive within the industry. The results of a study with 126 large organisations showed that the employees who believed they were getting a competitive salary were more productive and had higher morale, and customer satisfaction was improved, too. But since the wage costs are often the highest single operating cost of an organisation, paying too much will either make the company's products too expensive compared to the competition or make the business unprofitable (Robbins & Judge, 2022, pp. 156-157). Unless the whole industry has managed to obtain great profit margins, in which situations motivating people to stay in the company and grow professionally and "luring in" the best professionals from outside with higher pay than competitors, and slightly compromising this considerable profit margin temporarily, could lead potentially to a competitive edge through improved quality of work and customer satisfaction, which can bring the profit margin back to the previous level despite the higher pay levels. And paying this higher salary might sometimes even be cheaper to the company than paying a lower salary. After all, more work experience in the job and increased competence means there's less need to spend time for learning on the go, and less "rookie mistakes", increasing the efficiency and productivity of the whole organisation, as well as improving the working atmosphere. The latter is based on the feeling of being appreciated by the employer (author's experience).

Another aspect of pay is rewarding, for example through bonuses. Individual performance assessments and rewarding might interfere with high-performing teams. Therefore, a hybrid rewarding system, rewarding both individual performance and the performance of the complete team or organisation, brings the importance of the outcome of the team effort into attention. Group-based assessments, sharing of the profits and small-group rewards together with positive feedback do increase the team effort and commitment. However, bias and discrimination must be avoided for this to work (Robbins & Judge, 2022, p. 189).

This also applies to the implementation of Total Cost of Ownership. Aligning the reward criteria to encourage teamwork for one common goal, both within a team or function and cross-functionally, is crucial for TCO efforts to succeed. When teamwork for common goals is emphasized in the rewarding criteria, we people look for ways to reach these goals instead of prioritizing our own areas of responsibility at the expense of the big picture. The opposite situation, in which individualistic behaviour is encouraged through individualistic incentives, can even lead to "deconstruction" of the team, frustration and even added turnover because of a compromised team spirit, all of which also increase the total TCO of running the business (author's own experience). Reward strategies and the related implementation processes should stem from the business strategy of the company. Successful reward management is based on the values of the organisation, helping to enact them. Reward policies must also be in line with the culture and strategic goals of the organisation (Armstrong & Murlis, 2007, pp. 4-5).

8.6   Negotiations and TCO

Negotiating is almost always part of everyday work in business. We negotiate both inside the organisation with our workmates, foremen and other internal stakeholders, as well as externally with our customers and suppliers, sometimes also with other external stakeholders. TCO and negotiations have several mutual effects and utilization possibilities, and in this section, we shall cover the relationship of TCO and both internal and external negotiations. John Hermarij in his work (Hermarij, 2021, p. 521) defines the actions of negotiation as:

- understanding the interests of all parties
- developing sufficient options to satisfy all needs
- designing an acceptable strategy to achieve our objectives
- reaching an agreement, which is in line with our objectives
- exploiting all commercial opportunities.

This is important, especially understanding the interests of all parties and developing sufficient options to satisfy all needs, because only then we can reach a win-win (Säkkinen, 2024). Win-win is in general preferred in almost all management literature. Win-win is a collection of small compromises that lead to a situation in which all parties perceive the outcome as fair. This fosters a good working relationship between the parties. However, not all negotiations can be win-win; price negotiations are dividing by nature. Furthermore, what's important is that all parties feel at the end of the negotiation that they have benefited from it and their interests are included in the contract in the best possible way (Hermarij, 2021, pp. 530-531).

This kind of negotiation targets and results are also beneficial for TCO, mostly because of fostering a good relationship between the parties. When all contract parties have a good relationship with each other, they trust each other, and this trust makes the collaboration more fluent. Additionally, when the contracting parties trust each other, they tend to have a more open atmosphere to talk openly and honestly about potential issues in a project, for example, and to propose required changes and discuss the alternatives for different technical solutions more openly. TCO can also be utilized in achieving a win-win. For example, even if a supplier candidate has very high initial investments in the quotation, the operating, maintenance and disposal or recycling costs may be low enough to offset this difference in the initial investments by such a margin, that the supplier candidate with the highest initial investment turns out to be eventually the cheapest alternative. If the supplier candidate can present this convincingly, even backed up with calculations, it is possible to reach a win-win even with the highest initial investments between the competing quotations (author's experience).

8.7   Safety and TCO

Besides contributing to our hierarchy of needs, as discussed in the section 8.2, our physical safety at work and the company finances go hand in hand in several aspects. After all, a workday missed by a regular employee, either the employee being substituted by someone else or the work not being done, usually means additional expenses. But here we talk about unplanned days off, focusing on sick leaves due to issues related to working conditions, injuries and so on. Not every day off, such as annual vacation, is away from productivity. We people are not machines, who can operate almost 24/7.

Human health is in general strongly related to security, safety and environment. Security includes vulnerabilities of systems, risks at work, potential threats, countermeasures against risks and threats and the extent to which we can trust being secured. *Safety* concerns protecting people from physical and psychological harm. When assessing the environmental impact, we:

- make environmental impact a part of our decision-making
- prevent or mitigate negative effects
- retain functions of natural systems and
- provide information (Hermarij, 2021, pp. 668-673).

All these aspects are important also for TCO. Thanks to the increased health and safety consciousness in business, companies simply cannot afford to neglect these things anymore. Not only are security and environmental aspects an integral part of the image of any modern company, but good working conditions are also such a common expectation in many countries and even continents nowadays that without fulfilling those expectations it's hard to get the professional workforce in. Not only that, but any serious physical injury or any other serious harm, especially when causing something permanent, is expensive to the company. When an employee gets into a serious accident, there are multiple internal and external stakeholders involved in the investigation work, such as foremen, managers, HSE personnel, directors and external health and safety officials. Local inspection officials and even police and law enforcement officials, too, in the cases of serious neglect. Not only are these cases bad for the reputation of the company, but in general, working in an unsafe environment eats away the productivity of the workforce at least via two "paths". Firstly, having to constantly beware of safety risks does not enable workers to fully focus on the work at hand, not allowing them to utilize their full capacity in the work itself. Working under the constant risk of an injury or other severe harm may put workers under such a heavy mental load that they cannot "climb up to the further levels" of the hierarchy of needs. After all, innovation, development and other similar phenomena happen mostly on the top levels of the hierarchy of needs (Herrity, 2024). We cannot innovate if we must fear for our own safety. And this is why I personally recommend first making the working conditions as safe as possible in every single way, given the nature of the work, and only then focusing on the protective equipment required once the workplace itself is as safe as possible. Of course, this doesn't mean that, for example, the noise level should be the number 1 selection criteria for the new production equipment. It would be naïve to suggest such. However, taking unnecessary health and safety risks rarely saves money in the long run, no matter how lucrative it might make the initial purchase price (author's experience). And this does not involve only the physical safety and security against immediate physical injury. There are also other physical factors, such as air quality, temperature, surrounding noise level and so on. Working in poor working conditions also puts us under immense psychological stress, increasing the likelihood of burnout and other psychological harm under heavy workloads. What also adds to this psychological aspect is poor leadership. If the typical answer by the leader of the team in the face of any resistance is something like "Are you declining from work?" or "There's the door. You can walk out if you don't like it", the team members lose the feeling of emotional safety and most likely won't either express their true feelings or collaborate well with the leader. And this lowers the productivity of the entire team (author's experience).

TCO can also be utilized if needing to convince decision-makers to invest in health and safety. There are a lot of statistics available about average costs of a sick leave and an injury, and these often outweigh perceived cost savings from taking these risks. Of course, there have been a lot of cases in which, despite this, the company has knowingly chosen to retain even a lethal risk in its product rather than fixing it, after making the calculation concerning which is cheaper, fixing the risk or just "letting it be". For example, more than one well-known automotive manufacturer has chosen this path, leading to well-deserved scandal on the topic (author's view).

8.8   Personnel turnover and TCO

"Employee turnover is the percentage of employees that leave your organization during a given time period." (Shweta, 2024). Turnover of the personnel affects company finances both directly and indirectly, especially when it concerns a big number of people. There are many kinds of turnover:

- involuntary and voluntary turnover, meaning whether the employee leaves the company of his or her own will or not
- functional and dysfunctional turnover, meaning whether the employee's departure becomes beneficial for the employer or not
- avoidable and unavoidable turnover, meaning whether the employee is leaving the company for something that will happen, no matter what the employer does or, for example, due to poor management, in which case the resignation can still be "prevented" if management acts fast with corrective actions (Dwesini, 2019).

Turnover is affected, for example, by how much the work interferes with family and community satisfactions as much as receiving the need satisfactions at work (Ross & Zander, 1957). The hierarchy of needs was discussed in an organisational context in Chapter 8.2 of this book. In this section of the book, however, we shall focus on the two "opposite extremes of the personnel turnover within the context of TCO: Big layoffs and personnel cuts, also known as change negotiations, and big recruitment campaigns, which both have TCO implications.

8.8.1 Downsizing and layoffs & TCO

Here in Finland and in many other countries, there is currently an enormous quantity of experienced job applicants because of layoffs and job cuts (downsizing) that have been very common in several industries during this and the past few years. When encountering a big reduction in the needed production volumes, it is very common that manufacturing companies resort to layoffs and even personnel cuts, meaning contract terminations. The purpose and target of these actions are to cut the costs immediately to counter the negative financial effects of the reduced revenue. However, do big and frequent layoffs or even personnel cuts save money in the long run, or even in short-term, as much as intended to? We shall find out based on the research on the topic.

Aside from job cuts and layoffs due to the reduced order intake resulting from an economic downturn, downsizing can be done with the aim of having a leaner organisation structure that is focused completely on adding value to the end product. This production and management philosophy is known as lean enterprise. In this philosophy, the value is determined based on how much the customer is willing to pay for the product. Downsizing can also be carried out with the aim to retain the skills, competences and talents required for the company to achieve its strategic objectives and goals (Halton, 2024). And sometimes temporary layoffs or downsizing, which is focused on permanent reduction of employees, can help the company avoid bankruptcy during difficult times. However, to me, this always begs the question: Could the company have avoided the need to resort to these measures in the first place by utilizing its employees and non-human resources more smartly? After all, multiple studies have shown that these measures have their flip side that can more than offset the seemingly made savings in the salary and software license budgets, for example (author's experience). Downsizing may even go against the intentions of avoiding bankruptcy through reduced productivity, lowered customer satisfaction and worsened employee morale so badly that it even increases the likelihood of bankruptcy. Losing employees with valuable information may reduce innovation in an organisation, and the remaining employees often have to cope with increased workload and stress. This gives very little time to learn new skills, and all this together may very well negate any theoretical gain in productivity. Additionally, losing trust in the management reduces employee engagement and loyalty (Halton, 2024). And even though this is definitely the case with downsizing, constant layoffs have many similar effects on the organisation. Moreover, constant layoffs and job cuts eat into one of the basic organisational needs of human beings: the feeling of security. After all, if we have to worry about losing our jobs due to layoffs or budget cuts, it will be more challenging for us to find the motivation to move towards performing at our highest level (Herrity, 2024). This was also shown for example in the study conducted in Los Angeles and Washington in 2018 (Stunk et al., 2018), showing that the teachers affected by the layoff process became less productive than those who didn't have to experience the threat of losing their jobs. Additionally, those who were first laid off and then hired back were showing less productivity during the first two years after layoff. Furthermore, layoffs can be even traumatising to those experiencing them, while the ones remaining are in working in a "survivor mode". Layoffs are tough on leaders, too, who have to experience the conflict between caring for the team and working hard to get the best out of the team and having to choose who stays and who doesn't. This may bring the leaders to question the core values of their employer. Moreover, layoffs can be damaging on customer relations, too, especially if the key contacts of the customer are laid off (Kennemer, 2016).

Since layoffs rarely yield the targeted cost savings in the long run, why are they such a commonplace? The incentive criteria for the CEOs are one of the key drivers here, along with the perceived potential for cost savings. For example, a study conducted from 1993 to 1999 (Brookman et al., 2007) showed that the CEOs of companies announcing layoffs receive 22,8% more total pay on average during the year following the layoffs compared to CEOs from other companies.

But could there be an alternative approach? Could there be a good reason for some companies to have adopted a zero-layoff policy? For example, Appinventiv, a global mobile application development agency, chose to retain job-safety for 99,5% of its employees during 2023. This boosted employee morale because the company showed that it considers the humans in its organisation one of its critical pillars of success. In addition, Appinventiv increased bonuses, incentives and variable compensation to reward exceptional performance. This, combined with the upskilling of the employees both through technical certifications and non-technical trainings focused on soft skills and leadership, helped the company to increase its revenue from 490 million INR, approximately 5,36 million € (xe.com, 2024) in 2020 to 1,44 billion INR, approximately 15,76 million €, (xe.com, 2024), very nearly tripling the revenue in that time period (Business Today, 2024). Other companies that have implemented a zero-layoff policy include, for example, Southwest Airlines and Barry-Wehmiller. Both companies consider serving their employees as the top priority because when employees are served well, and they feel appreciated, they serve the customer well. This drives the business and benefits the stakeholders (Sinek, 2019, pp. 284-285).

8.8.2 Major recruitments and TCO

When business is booming for a company, it might need to hire hundreds of workers, or even more, in a short period. And even though this is a positive challenge in a way, it is a major challenge. After all, hiring a lot of workers also requires a lot from the personnel already working in the company. HR professionals, directors and managers need to arrange tons of job interviews. A lot of time needs to be arranged to read through the applications and CVs. Often recruiters also get a huge number of phone calls, both from potential applicants and recruitment companies, offering their services. This also sets an enormous challenge to upper management: Can the personnel already existing in the company even handle all this work alongside other work tasks? All this work, and recruitment campaigns, adds up to costs (author's experience).

There are several direct costs related to recruiting. And the more people are being hired, the more it usually requires effort from the current personnel in the company. The direct costs include things like:

- advertising
- screening and assessments
- onboarding and training.

And if the newcomer doesn't fit in for one reason or another and the working contract is soon terminated on the employer's or employee's initiative, the entire recruitment process has to be restarted. Additionally, there are indirect costs, such as lost productivity or business opportunity costs if major positions remain vacant due to not being able to find a suitable candidate (Shields, 2023). Other indirect costs include reduced time allowed for daily tasks for those participating in the recruitment process from the employer's side, effort done for recruitment permits and potentially required arrangements to conduct the interviews. Speaking of permits, also working permits and other required legal paperwork is one of the hidden costs of recruitment. One potentially major indirect cost is also related to lost productivity or business opportunity: If the whole recruitment process is so heavy that it cannot respond to the sudden need for a recruitment, a position is forced to be left vacant until it will even be possible to hire a good candidate to fill it (author's experience).

But despite the potential cost of lost productivity or lost business opportunities, it often still isn't worth it to rush to "just get someone". Hiring individuals who don't suit the role or are so far off from the company culture that they don't ft in, might lead to having an ineffective workforce, increased employee turnover, affecting the company culture negatively, damaging the reputation of the company or missing opportunities for growth and innovation and having a competitive disadvantage (Shields, 2023). When speaking about how well someone suits the company culture and the team, a lot of the study of this field speaks about organisational fit. And the organisational fit is very important both for the newcomer and the team he or she joins, and for the whole organisation. Not only does a good organisational fit make it easier for the newcomer to settle into the new team, but it also makes the start of collaboration more efficient, along with many other benefits (author's experience).

Aside from the direct and indirect cost effect related to the recruitment process, big and quick-paced recruitment campaigns may also include other hidden costs. A quickly and greatly growing organisation must ensure that sharing internal information will work effectively despite having to reach out the much bigger quantities of people than before. In businesses where secrecy policies and non-disclosure agreements are a part of everyday work, extra attention will have to be paid to avoid slipping out business secrets or information about potential new customers even internally (author's experience). If this happens, it can have very damaging consequences for the reputation of the company and for the relationship with potential customers.

I could conclude the whole section in one sentence: It is very worthwhile to plan and execute recruitment campaigns thoroughly, as well as doing everything to make sure the internal processes and ways of working will suit the new situation of having much more people in the organisation than before (author's view).

8.9   Work location and TCO

Basically, the work location can be divided into two major categories within this context: working at the office or remotely. The third category is so-called hybrid work, in which part of the work week is spent at the office and part remotely. Even though there are many other kinds of workplaces, too, apart from the office, it's office work where the option to work also remotely is mostly viable, which is why in this section we compare the two and the hybrid between them within the context of TCO implications, both to the employing company and to the employee.

Firstly, when workers work full time remotely instead of full time in the office, they save a considerable amount of money, which consists of saving mostly on commuting and meals. One survey showed that full-time office workers spend $440 more per month ($863 vs. $423) on these expenses. If we multiply this by 12 months, it becomes 5 280 dollars per year (Cagnassola, 2022). Depending on the national or regional legislation, it might be also possible to apply for a tax reduction based on having done much of the work at home, as a compensation for using the electricity, network and so on at home for the purposes of work (author's experience). On the other hand, isolation of remote work can lead to the feeling of loneliness, which can increase stress and significantly affect the employee performance (Montañez, 2024). And if the employee is achievement-oriented, he or she might get even more stressed from the feeling of lowered performance at work. And this stress requires a relieving method, which is different for different people. For many people, hobbies are an excellent way to relieve stress, and if the hobby is expensive, the savings from commuting for work and meals at work may very well become more than offset by the spending at the hobby (author's view). Many studies have also shown the various negative effects that stress has on our eating habits, and the resulting negative health effects add up also to our expenses in the long run, when continued for long periods of time. All this works very much in the principles of the Total Cost of Ownership: The apparent saving turns into an added expense (author's experience).

Remote work has its pros and cons from an employer's point of view, too. The feeling of flexibility offered by the chance to work remotely may boost the productivity of some employees. And of course, we people are different; some find the calm of home a more efficient surrounding in which to focus on complex tasks, if having a quiet environment at home during the working day is possible (author's experience). I also like to work occasionally from home when there are tasks that require long periods of focusing alone. Then again, working from home can also be taxing on employee productivity. Many studies show that, for most employees, productivity decreases when working from home. However, this does not directly result from working from home but from remarkable changes in working patterns when working remotely. Many employees spend more time in shorter and larger group meetings than they would when working in the office. And this leads to less "focus time", which is the working time uninterrupted by meetings or calls. Additionally, when working remotely, employees tend to narrow down their social network, and the chance for direct contact with their manager also reduces. All this together leads to reduced productivity, which shows that coordination and communication are more difficult when working remotely (Gibbs et al., 2023).

Working at the office also has its TCO implications both for the employees and employers. Direct monetary effects on employees include commuting and meals if there is no affordable meal arranged by the workplace. Then again, contrary to remote work, the more natural need for humans to interact face-to-face can be fulfilled when working together in the office. When working remotely, that need can be partially fulfilled when having the cameras on during meetings and calls, but it's not the same. And as discussed in Section 8.2, fulfilling our needs contributes to the TCO of the entire business, too. When working remotely, tasks requiring a lot of teamwork tend to become more efficient, too. In the manufacturing industry, such tasks may include project planning, planning of the production concept and cross-functional review meetings. And one of the most important effects on the change of productivity from remote to office is that we humans tend to focus on the actual topic at hand when having the meeting face-to-face instead of trying to multitask during the meeting. The latter takes away the focus from both, following the meeting and work tasks, which can lead to both being done poorly (author's experience).

I sincerely wish I could give an answer once and for all to the currently "roaming" question of which is more efficient and productive, working remotely or working in the office. But since all people and all working positions are somewhat different, that would be impossible. What I can recommend instead is to adapt the model of working location to the nature of work, the wishes of the team and what needs to be accomplished at work and by what means. Additionally, working remotely and working in the office require different approaches to managing things and, especially, to leading people.

8.10   Organisational silos and TCO

"A *silo mentality is the unwillingness to share information or knowledge between employees or across different departments within a company*" (Kenton, 2020). It also refers to the use of software in which information cannot be shared because of the limitations in the software. This is known as a silo system. The silo mentality is seen as a top-down issue, stemming from the competition between senior managers, directors and so on. One of the "symptoms" of this silo thinking is the protective attitude towards information, and this attitude spreads downwards in the organisational hierarchy. Most siloed ways of working can be perceived between the employees from "competing departments", whose duties somewhat overlap. However, the silo mentality doesn't always occur as a protective attitude towards information and other egoistic approaches. It can also come from a narrow vision, being unable to set a person's own work into the context of the bigger picture of the respective business (Kenton, 2020). Among employees, for example in a project, this can also occur as competition between different activity teams within the same sub-project, often at the expense of the big picture, potentially causing budget overruns and delays (author's experience).

Siloed ways of working can lead to functions having to work with inaccurate or outdated information due to the hindered flow of information. Additionally, the phenomenon can worsen the working morale of the organisation when the organisation recognizes it but cannot find ways to do anything about it. Silo mentality can also reduce the value delivered to the customer and even decrease the profitability of business operations (Kenton, 2020).

And this leads us to the first aspect of the connection between organisational silos and TCO: The siloed approach to working is, in many ways, the opposite of the purpose of TCO. After all, Total

Cost of Ownership is ultimately all about cross-functional collaboration and good stakeholder management, aiming to reduce the total lifecycle costs instead of sub-optimising between various budgets. In a siloed organisation, where selfish approaches and highly individualistic incentives are considered normal, a lot of time and money is wasted in the battle of egos, arguing over pointless topics and wasting everyone's time. This can occur in so many ways, but some of the most common ones are:

- partial optimisation between different budgets

- conflicting demands from different managers and directors

- self-centred approaches, focusing merely on the success of everyone's own area of responsibility on the expense of the big picture

- no willingness to find lean methods benefiting everyone but always "reinventing the wheel"

- making approval of anything a show of power and

- unnecessary additional approval phases just to satisfy the hunger for power by decision-makers (author's experience).

And all this is a waste of time and money both directly and indirectly; directly through a lot of non-value adding work and indirectly through added frustration and stress and worsened morale of the organisation. And thus, worsening the TCO of running the business.

And how can the silo effect be countered? TCO work can help with this, because it requires collaboration between different functions, sharing expertise and bringing people from different functions closer together to work on the same goal. On the other hand, the silo effect can also be affected positively through successful team building and a more collective approach to incentives. In practice, the latter means that the rewards, such as bonuses, are at least majorly yielded from the success of the whole organisation instead of the success of only a small part of it or of a single individual. For example, rewarding the project manager for the under-run of the project budget at the expense of the total lifecycle costs of the product itself can be destructive for business profitability. The bonus criteria may also be quite conflicting; if the project manager is at the same time rewarded for the under-run of the project budget and for the profitability of the company or business unit, these two targets might turn against each other if one happens on the expense of the other. This may frustrate the project manager, lowering his or her job engagement and working morale, which eats into profitability further. One important aspect is also the personality traits of the CEO, given that in many cases, the silo effect has spread top down. The traits such as conscientiousness, openness to experience and extraversion, along with things like age and tenure in management, can reduce the appearance of organisational silos (Mouta & Meneses, 2021).

8.11   Lazy thinking and TCO

"We all like to think we're open-minded, but the reality is our brains are hard-wired to prefer information that aligns with what we already know and think." Presenting a new idea that goes against the current state of affairs can make people feel uncomfortable, especially if the idea is unforeseen, unproven and previously unknown in the organisation. A fresh idea also requires more effort. New ideas also get judged against the confidence of the person presenting them. Research has also shown that extroverts might be more easily considered knowledgeable, even if it's the shy introvert who knows more on the subject. In business, it's also more beneficial to be deliberate, careful and to consider alternatives and to counter emotional reasoning and biases instead of focusing only on one alternative and reacting strongly with emotion (Lipkin, 2022).

The former way of thinking is also required constantly when implementing and utilizing Total Cost of Ownership. After all, the whole point of it is to compare alternative options in a financial context, even options that are very different from each other in principle. And even though TCO is already several decades old in its early forms of the concept, it isn't very widespread, especially beyond procurement and supply chain management. It is important to acknowledge this when introducing TCO in an organisation, because it goes against the ways of sub-optimising between budgets and making decisions based on how the decisions affect the decision-makers and their immediate surroundings. Acknowledging this also helps to prepare for potential change resistance that is always occurring in one way or the other, at least from some people, when trying to introduce and implement major changes in ways of working that people are already used to.

And I do not say this to be negative, far from it. But it would be unrealistic to expect to be able to introduce a new idea going against the status quo and everyone accepting it full-hearted immediately. Lazy thinking is also something that must be avoided when utilizing TCO in any context, because in many cases several viable alternatives can be found by thinking outside the box. Even though in industrial projects we might be used to comparing several similar solutions to each other, sometimes an alternative approach is better. These different solutions are not always the most obvious ones, which means we might need to exert more effort in coming up with them. Then again, some ideas that feel like out of the box for even most of the team, might come naturally to some members (author's experience), which is why group diversity is one of the major ways of countering lazy thinking in an organisation, along with sharing the information and promoting innovation, for example (Lipkin, 2022).

PART C – Organisational function context of TCO

And so, we arrive at the last major leg of this journey: organisational function context of Total Cost of Ownership. In this part, we shall discuss how TCO is connected with different functions of a big manufacturing and engineering company. These TCO implications apply in pretty much any industrial company, but of course not all companies contain all the functions described in this part C of this book. And my intention is not to emphasize the singularity of different functions in a business, far from it. On the contrary: When we understand what and how different functions can contribute to the optimisation of the whole Total Cost of Ownership of the whole company and how different functions can benefit from the TCO work, it encourages different functions to work for the benefit of the whole company, utilizing the best expertise in each. After all, there are very few phenomena as destructive to the optimisation of the Total Cost of Ownership of the entire company as different functions "playing solo", indifferent to each other and only considering themselves and their budgets in their decision-making. Additionally, when the management understands the implications of TCO to different business functions, it can utilize the benefits of TCO more effectively.

Let's unroll the map once more and head on to the waves of an ocean that is Total Cost of Ownership.

9 PRODUCT DEVELOPMENT AND TCO

Product development, or R&D, as this function is sometimes called, is responsible for product research, product development, product updates and quality control of the product. Sometimes the product development department is also responsible for the market research to understand if there is a market for the new product (Indeed Editorial Team, 2024). Product development is also a major point of the Total Cost of Ownership of the product, because many of the decisions made in the product development phase can have a huge impact on how costly the product will be to manufacture and transport, as well as which suppliers will be capable of manufacturing parts of the product (author's experience). Product development is also increasingly recognised as a crucial source of competitive advantage (Noble & Kumar, 2010).

In this chapter we shall focus on the product development function and its TCO implications, applied in cost engineering point of view. This is one of those chapters where I can apply my words in the Foreword section: I am a student of this topic. I do not come from a product development background, although I have had a small bit of training as an introduction to the topic but having observed many aspects of major industrialisation projects from cost engineer's point of view, and keeping TCO in mind, I still feel that I have a lot to give to this topic. So, let's carry on our fascinating journey together.

9.1 New product development process and TCO

To understand product development as a function and the TCO implications of product development, we first must understand the new product development process, NPD. Which is why I'm starting this chapter with this topic. If we don't understand it, we cannot apply any other knowledge to it.

9.1.1 New product development process (NPD)

The categorisation of the process of developing a new product varies a bit from one source of information to another, although the main points are the same even if in different words, but to me the following one seems a bit more familiar from the little experience I have. However, based on my experience, the new product development process is not done in a strict waterfall, finishing first one phase and then moving to another; many phases are started as soon as there's enough input from the previous one:

1. Idea generation
2. Idea screening
3. Concept testing
4. Prototyping
5. External refinement and testing
6. Perfecting the design and preparing for production
7. Preparing for potential issues and solutions
8. Commercialisation
9. Post-launch activities
10. Reviewing the performance of the new product (Seasia Infotech, 2022).

Besides not being a strict waterfall, sometimes there are setbacks that require returning to previous phases, which is why new product development could in a way also be understood as a cycle, in which moving to the next phase without returning to the start or some part of the previous steps happens only when each step has been verified to be successfully completed.

Idea generation is the first step, because we first need to have an idea to start working on it. Understanding the needs of the potential customers is the key driver in this phase. Some ways to boost idea generation include encouraging customers to give suggestions, conducting market research, brainstorming new ideas, searching for fresh ideas on the market and obtaining feedback of competitors' services and products.

During idea screening, the following questions are typically asked:

➢ Is launching a new product really required?
➢ Can the existing marketing network be utilized to sell the product?
➢ Is it possible to utilize the existing equipment to manufacture the new product?
➢ When is the new product expected to be profitable?

For an idea to pass the screening, the answers to these questions must be affirmative. This phase is crucial to avoid hugely expensive product failures.

In the concept testing phase, the ideas are presented to real people outside the product development process itself. The purpose is to find out which ideas are worth proceeding with and which ones should be abandoned. This helps in understanding how the ideas would resonate with the target audience.

In the prototype phase, a handcrafted, 3D-printed physical replication or a digital mock-up might be enough for presentation. The prototype should be fully functional before testing it. To discover potential design defects or areas to improve, the expected production process should be mimicked as much as possible.

Upon approaching the launch phase, the new product is distributed to trusted customers or partners for external testing, sometimes called beta testing, to get feedback to guide in improving the design. At this phase, the product should be functionally as close to the final product as possible. This phase can also benefit from functional models built by the manufacturing department based on the prototype.

The results from beta testing are utilized when preparing the product design for production. Preparing for production starts once a feasible level of product maturity is reached. Aside from keeping the end user and the direct customer, marketing must be involved in the process to hone the functioning models to suit customer desires. Marketing also provides the sales forecasts of the product to guide the production capacity planning. In this phase, the production process and surrounding aspects and functions must also be honed ready for the mass production.

When preparing for potential issues and solutions, all aspects of the product must be considered before releasing it to the market. Especially the following points must be considered:

➢ How we set up and monitor the whole production process?

➢ Which manufacturing partners we can select to assist with production or post-launch activities?

➢ How can we integrate the product into the existing supply chain?

➢ How to package the product, keeping both functionality and brand marketing in mind?

➢ Which product variants we need to make available and how many each?

Marketing needs to raise product awareness, generate leads and increase demand at this point. Additionally, all product literature, distributor and customer service training, and lead-generating materials, such as advertisements, must be planned and created. The external distribution channels and internal sales team must be involved in the development of these materials to help them accept and utilize the materials. After all, poor sales channel preparation is one of the major causes of a poor product launch.

If the test marketing is successful, the company will roll out the product on a big scale. This phase is called commercialisation. The product is produced in great volumes, and mass media is utilized for the product promotion purposes.

Post-launch activities involve a lot of effort from several internal stakeholders, when a new product has been launched. Sales, marketing, customer service and engineering must work together to respond to early adopter concerns and increase customer satisfaction. Also, potential faults must be resolved. Additionally, developing and launching a new product may take years, depending on the industry, so it is often started only in a matter of months or a year after the launch of the previous product.

In the last phase, the performance of the new product is reviewed with customer research, such as satisfaction surveys and marketing performance assessments. The latter one must answer the following questions:

- *"Is the new product well received by customers?*
- *Is there a similar new product on the market from your competitors?*
- *Is there a lot of demand, sales, and profit?*
- *Is the marketing team satisfied with the new product's revenue?*
- *Is the after-sales service satisfactory to the customers?*
- *Is the commission paid to the middlemen satisfactory?*
- *Is the marketing manager adjusting the marketing mix in response to environmental changes?"* (Seasia Infotech, 2022).

9.1.2 NPD and TCO

Now that we understand the basics of the new product development process, we can start thinking about how it is tied to the TCO of the product. Very much, it turns out. All the decisions made during the product development process have a major impact on the Total Cost of Ownership of the product, affecting mostly manufacturing, supply chain and aftermarket maintenance services. These add up to the product TCO both directly and indirectly. Design for manufacturing and assembly will be discussed more closely in Section 9.6, but the product design affects many aspects of manufacturing costs. Every single component needs to be joined to the product somehow, and every added process phase adds to the manufacturing costs. This is why so-called over-engineering, in which the product is more complex than it needs to be to fulfil all the requirements, must be avoided. That said, avoiding over-engineering is far from a synonym to low quality. Sometimes lack of over-engineering in the product can even add up to the feel of quality perceived by the customer, because over-engineering often means additional components and added complexity, which means more complexity in the aftermarket product maintenance and repairs, and potentially added faults in the product, more precisely in the additional components.

Product design also affects the supply chain in multiple ways. The packaging of the product is greatly affected by the external dimensions, shape and, for example, pointy shapes in the product. Over-engineering of the product has negative TCO effects in the supply chain, too, because added components add weight and size, which means more transportation capacity is required for the same quantity of products, which increases transportation costs.

Aside from the complexity of the product and the complexity and quantity of its components, and its size and shape, also the materials used in the product affect the manufacturing and supply chain related costs. For example, the selection of certain materials can limit the availability of different options for the methods of joining the components together. And this is why overachieving on the technical specifications of the product might just be a waste of time and money, at least if it doesn't bring any added value to the direct customer and end user. After all, even if the direct customer differs from the end user, the demand from end users is affected by the perceived price-to-quality, meaning value, which has a major impact on the demand from the direct customer.

But the product development department mustn't be left alone to figure out the solutions to dilemmas related to the Total Cost of Ownership of manufacturing the product and the related operations. Simultaneous Engineering, which is discussed more in detail in Section 9.7, is a powerful method for this purpose (author's experience). And if you, dear reader, find my work in this book useful and interesting enough to want to read more, perhaps you can read also further about product development and simultaneous engineering and their TCO implications someday in my works or elsewhere.

But before we proceed to the target costing and its Japanese application, Genka kikaku, I want to give a warning: Pushing forward in the new product development process despite potentially severe issues in the product, refusing to take any steps backwards, has catastrophic effects on the TCO of the whole product. These effects, especially when combined with organisational issues, can become so bad that they can even bring down entire companies, all the way to insolvency and bankruptcy.

And all this can happen to any company, but especially to early-stage firms, where financial resources, amount of personnel and quantity of existing products is very limited (Marion & Meyer, 2011). Because the survival and growth of these companies absolutely depends on the successful product commercialization of new products, industrial design and cost engineering are critical to early-stage companies.

9.2   Target costing & Genka kikaku

Now that we understand the basics of the product development process and its connection with the Total Cost of Ownership of the product lifecycle, we shift our focus to the powerful cost management methods. After all, we need to have something concrete to achieve the targeted cost reductions. So, let's start with the target costing and its somewhat similar Japanese counterpart, Genka kikaku.

9.2.1 History

Early approaches to target costing date as far back as the early 20th century at Ford Motor Company in United States and in the development of the Volkswagen Beetle in Germany in 1930s. In both cases, one of the key drivers of product design was the targeted selling price of the vehicle. However, the full form of the target-costing approach began after World War II, when resources were scarce. In this time, the concept of maximising desirable product attributes while minimising the product costs was developed in the US. This concept became known as Value Engineering. Japanese companies then adopted this technique to withstand the stiff competition in the domestic markets. Value engineering was combined with the idea of trying to reduce the product costs as early in the product lifecycle as possible. In Japan this combination became known as Genka kikaku, which in the Western world became known as target costing, even though the original meaning is "target cost management" according to the Japan Cost Society, defined in their annual meeting of 1995, 32 years after it was first applied at Toyota in 1963 (Feil et al., 2004).

However, it wasn't until 1990s when Genka kikaku was started to be applied more widely within Japanese companies because of several major economic effects on the country through the bursting of the economic bubble in 1990 and 1991, the drastic changes in exchange rates between U.S. dollar and Japanese yen in 1993-1995, bringing down the profitability in exports, and the long recession caused by the finance sector crisis (Feil et al., 2004).

And why am I explaining all this, even though I haven't done so this extensively in any other section, in most sections not at all? In my opinion, understanding the connection between target costing and value engineering helps us to combine the two powerful methods in the aim for improved profitability in the manufacturing industry. And understanding the historical background gives a context to why these methods were developed in the first place.

9.2.2 The Western and the Japanese way of target cost management

As we can already guess based on the development of target costing and value engineering, the Western and Japanese approaches to target costing differ from each other. In both applications, the process starts with market research followed by product characteristics. After this, however, the two become different. Whereas in the Western world a cycle of design, engineering and supplier pricing follows these phases until the desired cost level has been reached, the Japanese version resumes from product characteristics to the equation of

$target\ cost = planned\ selling\ price - desired\ profit$. This is then derived into target costs for each component concerning design, engineering and supplier pricing, after which both the Western and Japanese versions of target costing resume to manufacturing. Another major difference between the two is related to cost reduction work during the production phase. Whereas the Western countries seem to prefer periodic cost reductions in bigger steps, often through separate cost-saving programs, the Japanese companies prefer constant and incremental cost reduction also known as Genka Kaizen (Feil et al., 2004). The main purpose of target costing, or Genka kikaku, is the realisation of customer expectations both in functionality and cost, which is why the customer input concerning both aspects is vital to the success of this process.

In practice, the Japanese approach to Target Cost Management, Genka kikaku, can be explained as "a tool to spend resources to right place respecting the voice of customer, R&D inputs, quality problems and cost reduction matters". In Genka kikaku, the fundamental question is "what is the right share of the product price in the eyes of the customer?" (Tasdeviren, 2016). In practice, this means putting more effort into the very features of the product that are also the most valued ones in the eyes and minds of the customers (author's remark). The input of Genka kikaku comes from:

- internal quality issues
- direct complaints or claims from the customers
- direct customer demands
- suggestions from employees or kaizen work and
- R&D (Tasdeviren, 2016).

However, even though the process of Genka kikaku sounds straightforward in theory, it doesn't mean that by following this process the target price is automatically achieved while retaining the desired level of profitability. To apply this concept successfully in a company, the underlying concept must be adopted first (Feil et al., 2004) throughout the organisation, and exactly the same statement holds true with TCO (author's experience). Even though in Western literature this is often disregarded, rather focusing on the related processes and techniques, the importance of management philosophy is highlighted in Toyota Production System (TPS), which focuses on techniques, systems and philosophy (Feil et al., 2004).

9.3   Value engineering in product development

Value Engineering (VE) and target costing are complementary methods, because one allows the correct identification of where cost reduction could be achieved, and the other one shows the cost targets that need to be reached to ensure the long-term profitability of the business (Ibusuki & Kaminski, 2007). To succeed in manufacturing high-quality products with reasonable production costs, a program of new product development must also contain projects that aim at enhancing the value to the customer by lowering product costs while retaining the functionality. As explained in Section 2.2 of this book, the same can be achieved by improving functionality while retaining a similar cost level. To reach the target-cost level defined during the product development process, Ibusuki and Kaminski (2007) propose a Value Engineering method that focuses on three distinct steps to maximise the cost reduction potential and to improve the quality, too:

- Concept-VE, focusing on the product concept and aiming at functional innovations
- Project-VE, focusing on the product and process design, aiming at cost improvements in this phase
- Validation-VE, focusing on the validation phase of the product and process, and in the production phase, focusing on the improvements of the built production process.

Out of the steps of Value Engineering presented above, the Concept-VE is concerned with the search for possible innovation in the product concept, before the quality, cost and investment requirements are set. While traditional value engineering is concerned with enhancing the value of an existing design, the benefit of Concept-VE lies in the value-adding potential by coming up with concepts that were not thought of previously. Thus, by incorporating a stage of innovation search into the product development process, the chance of developing revolutionary products increases (Ibusuki & Kaminski, 2007).

Meanwhile, Project-VE focuses on the search for added value during the product and process design phase. This is the most traditional aspect of value engineering, which focuses on enhancing the value of an existing design. Project-VE is done in six phases:

1. Preparation
   a. choose the product
   b. determine targets and
   c. form a work group and determine activities
2. Information
   a. obtain general information about the product being studied, e.g. details, costs and values
3. Analytic
   a. identify functions and their costs
   b. relate the functions and costs
   c. determine critical functions and
   d. formulate the problem
4. Creative
   a. obtain ideas
   b. select and grade the ideas
5. Judgement
   a. formulate and develop alternatives
   b. propose technical and economical solutions and
   c. decide on the best alternative
6. Planning
   a. present the proposed alternative
   b. plan the implementation and then implement the best alternative.

Validation-VE is all about enhancing the value of a product during its validation process. At this phase, the components of the main functions are identified, and prototypes are assembled. At this stage, the target is to enhance the value of the product by improving the functionality of the existing components without adding new ones.

Basically, the Validation-VE is focused on the reduction of material and process costs. This can be achieved, for example, through the reduction of the part quantity, designing smaller and lighter parts, using cheaper components and designing parts that don't require expensive manufacturing methods. Also, avoiding overachieving in the product quality compared to the initial targets is one method of cost reduction (Ibusuki & Kaminski, 2007). However, even though using cheaper components saves money directly for the manufacturer, these savings might not be so straightforward. "Saving in the wrong place" might lead to damage to the reputation of the business and its products, potentially leading to losing direct customers, reduced order intake and weakened chances of winning over new customers. Therefore, I recommend focusing on the avoidance of over-engineering by reducing the complexity of the products and by rationalising working and production processes rather than skipping on the product quality (author's view).

9.4   DTC & DTV – Design to Cost & Design to Value and TCO

The main idea of Design to Cost (DTC) is creating cost-effective product designs that help reach the predetermined and specified targets set for the manufacturing of products. Product development teams can lower the costs by using lower-performance components or removing unnecessary functionalities and features. The target of Design to Cost is to retain the competitive product price level. The production costs can also be further reduced by selecting cheaper materials. Design to Value (DTV), on the other hand, aims to maximise the use value of a new product for the customer or end user. For instance, this can be done by removing features or functionalities that don't bring any value to the end user or customer. Where DTV differs from DTC, the most is its focus on the performance, reliability and durability of a product rather than just meeting the target cost. According to McKinsey, DTV has the potential to improve both product quality and to increase the gross margins of manufacturing companies by 10-25%, in the automotive sector typically 12-15% (Hinshaw, 2023).

What is the connection of these concepts to TCO and what might be the key differences between the two concepts when reflected based on the TCO principles? First of all, the earlier the cost optimisation is done in the product lifecycle, the greater the results should be. I want to emphasize the word should, because making the cost optimisation early in the product life cycle does not guarantee the targeted positive results on the Total Cost of Ownership of the whole product; not to the company manufacturing it nor the direct customer or end user. If a decision to alter the design, to reduce the quality of one or more components, or selection of cheaper materials is done based only on minimising costs and trying to maximise the profit, this approach might "bite back". The reason behind this is quite simple: by saving in the wrong place, the risk of highly expensive corrective actions is greatly increased. These corrective actions include, among others:

- ➢ additional incoming quality checks to make sure the incoming material meets the requirements
- ➢ rework at one or more points in the manufacturing process
- ➢ expensive recall campaigns.

These are a considerable part of the Total Cost of Ownership of the whole product to the company. Additionally, there are other risks of hidden costs coming from gaining savings by lowering the product quality, mainly stemming from the damage to the image of the products resulting from the end users suffering from the poor product quality. Multiple breakdowns and possibly even dangerous faults can be very damaging to the reputation of the product itself and the company that produced it.

Moreover, a change in the product made based only on one cost aspect might very easily increase the costs elsewhere (author's experience). For example, if the component or a whole assembly belonging to a product contains critical or significant characteristics, it might be purposeful to produce the assembly in-house instead of outsourcing it to the lowest bidder. After all, critical characteristics of a product have a major impact on product quality, reliability and safety. These characteristics require special attention and control to ensure that they're consistent and that they comply with necessary requirements and specifications (Kowalczyk, 2024).

All in all, it is very important to identify the components that can be designed to cost and those that must be designed to value. Multiple factors affect this, such as the targeted customer segment, product type, technical requirements and customer expectations related to both the customer segment and the product type. For example, if a customer is looking to buy a very expensive car and he or she goes to test drive it in winter, only to discover that many of the features in the car don't work in winter when there might be snow, and that much of the interior squeaks or rattles when the weather is very cold, the customer will most likely not end up buying the product, choosing something else instead (author's experience). Furthermore, design to cost and the overall Total Cost of Ownership must never be prioritized over everything else to such an extreme that the safety of the end users is compromised for example by refusing to do the changes required to fix these even lethal design flaws afterwards. Instead, products should be designed to meet the quality requirements and expectations, to bring the value to the end users, and the focus on the design purely to cost should be limited to those components where it doesn't make a remarkable difference (author's view).

9.5 Product variants & TCO

"A product variant refers to a specific version or model of a product that differs slightly from other versions offered by the same manufacturer. These differences can include variations in features, specifications, colours, sizes, or any other attributes that distinguish one variant from another" (Gepard, 2024). The purpose of different product variants is to respond to the different needs and desires, as well as different technical and legal requirements in different market areas. For example, in the automotive industry, different regions have different vehicle homologation requirements. In some market areas, the driver's side of the vehicle differs from the one in some other areas. Other typical variants include exterior and interior colour, different equipment levels or individual optional extra equipment in the vehicle (author's experience).

The range of product variants affects also the TCO of the product, because the readiness to produce each variant of the product costs additional money both in production process investments and running costs, as well as in labour costs and other cost elements to engineer the solution required to produce these variants. For example, it might be much more expensive to arrange a choice from multiple colours of the product than having only one choice. However, additional costs are only one part of the financial equation of decision-making concerning what kind of and how many product variants to include. The other financial aspects related to this decision are concerned with the potential to bring additional profit. For example, would adding multiple colours of choice to the product range bring in more revenue than additional costs? This boils down to the forecasts of additional sales concerning these variants and the potential market price effect (author's experience).

Furthermore, the more complex the whole product is, sometimes the more complex the cost estimation can be because of multiple cost elements. For example, in products containing a lot of interconnected data systems, adding one more variant might require a lot of cross-checking to make sure the new option works with the rest of the product. Aside from this, having multiple variants naturally also increases the effort required in the product development process, as well as the cross-functional phases of it, such as market surveys to cover the earning potential of each product variant. Again, this doesn't necessarily mean that having more product variants is a bad thing as long as there is a good potential to make more revenue than offering these additional product variants costs. But this means that offering multiple choices to the customer without any understanding of the demand on the market will very likely diminish the profitability of the new product (author's view).

9.6   DfMA and TCO

"Design for Manufacture & Assembly (DfMA) is an engineering design methodology designers and manufacturers should use to minimise cost and increase the quality of product designs" (Engineering Product Design, 2024). The simplicity of manufacturing and the efficiency of assembly are at the centre of this design methodology, enabling faster, safer and more cost-effective manufacturing and assembly. Basically, DfMA consists of two methods: Design for Manufacturing (DFM) and Design for Assembly (DFA). The focus points of DFM are economical materials and production methods. The core principles of DFM are that:

➢ the parts must be designed to fit within the tolerance limits of the manufacturing process

➢ the part features must be within the capabilities of the chosen manufacturing process

➢ a designer must explore and improve all aspects of manufacturing, including e.g. fabrication, assembly, testing, shipping, procurement, repair of parts, service and assembly.

DFA focuses on minimising the quantity of assembly phases and reducing the assembly costs. Its principles are:

➢ Reduce the quantity and variety of part types.

➢ Aim to get rid of adjustment needs.

➢ Use guiding forms, holes etc. for self-aligning and self-locating of parts.

➢ Make sure the operators have a sufficient access and visibility to do the assembly work.

➢ Make sure the parts are easy to take from their packaging or shelves.

➢ Minimise the need for reorientations during the assembly process.

➢ Design parts so that they cannot be installed incorrectly.

➢ Either maximise part symmetry if possible or make parts asymmetric

➢ Eliminate further processing needs during the assembly process

➢ "Choose the appropriate economic scale for the process."

➢ "Standardise components and processes."

- ➢ Follow the "Black Box" principle of component procurement, describing what the component has to do, not how to achieve it.
- ➢ Minimise the system complexity (Engineering Product Design, 2024).

Both approaches are a great help in reducing the Total Cost of Ownership through remarkable cost reductions both in manufacturing and assembly processes. Moreover, the cost savings achieved through these methods tend to come from the considerable reductions in non-value adding work, which means the quality of the end product will not be compromised. On the contrary, it is very likely to be improved because of the reduction of unnecessary work phases. Additionally, the manufacturing- and assembly-friendly design reduces the human frustration related to the ease of making mistakes, which could have been avoided through smarter component design. And not only do the chances for potential mistakes reduce but also the number of workers can be reduced, which leads to further cost reductions. Of course, in the countries with very strict labour laws, this might lead to additional expenses concerning layoffs or contract terminations, which is another aspect of TCO (author's experience). And besides, even though the reduction of the workforce is often the default response to the reduced need of workers in the tasks where the amount of work was reduced, there are alternative solutions available. Especially in big companies, there is always somewhere work left undone, because the workforce is allocated only to handle the tasks related directly to the core business and related functions, as well as to the job descriptions related to this core business. This means that the decision makers might end up neglecting the assisting work needed to complete these tasks thoroughly. This is why "I dare to propose a wild idea": How about instead of automatically terminating the contracts of the workers who cannot be employed in their former tasks anymore, we train them to take care of other work opportunities existing within the same company? Not only does this bring variation to the careers of these people, but it also shows the employees that the company is so committed to them that it arranges them other productive work rather than "gets rid of them". This approach has a great potential to increase job engagement, job satisfaction and the sense of continuity of the work for the employees in the company, adding up to their feeling of job security, enabling them to "climb up" to higher levels in the hierarchy of organisational needs, as described in the section 8.2 of this book. Reaching the higher levels in the hierarchy of organisational needs has great potential for increasing the overall performance of these employees, and also boosting the morale of the whole organisation. And this cannot be a bad thing, can it? (author's view).

9.7 Simultaneous Engineering

Simultaneous engineering, also known as concurrent engineering, is a product design methodology that utilises an integrated product team consisting of design engineering, manufacturing engineering, and other functions, aiming to reduce the time required to bring the new product to the market. This requires extensive communication and coordination between all relevant stakeholders, but also has great potential to improve profitability. Well-executed simultaneous engineering does indeed shorten the time to market, giving competitive advantage, while poor execution only brings in additional issues and increased costs (Wikipedia, 2023). But more mutual benefits of SE and TCO will be discussed in Section 9.7.3

One of the common appearances of Concurrent Engineering is Early Simultaneous Influence (ESI), in which downstream functions, such as Manufacturing Engineering, have a concurrent instead of waterfall input to the upstream product development decision-making. One of organisational benefits of Simultaneous Engineering is that it helps to reduce the silo effect and heavy bureaucracy in big organisations. But this, and other organisational benefits of well-executed Simultaneous Engineering shall be looked upon in further detail in the section 9.7.2.

This section 9.7, even though short, is a very important consideration in new product development. If the new physical product is developed without understanding the principles and practices of manufacturing, the design of the product might become either very expensive or even impossible to manufacture. This leads to a lot of expensive rework in the manufacturing process, as well as in the product development. After all, badly executed or completely lacking Concurrent Engineering in a complex project including both new product development and industrialisation of the new product can lead to a complete disaster. In the worst financial case, this disaster of a project can even bring down an entire company.

9.7.1 Foundations of Simultaneous Engineering

"Concurrent engineering (CE) or concurrent design and manufacturing is a work methodology emphasizing the parallelization of tasks (i.e. performing tasks concurrently), which is sometimes called simultaneous engineering or integrated product development (IPD) using an integrated product team approach." When successful, concurrent engineering enables completing processes simultaneously, involving all disciplines. The need for product development processes to become more cost and time effective has led to the implementation of elements of concurrent engineering, such as cross-functional teams and consideration of downstream phases of the product lifecycle already in the design phase. The earliest adopters of simultaneous engineering include the aerospace industry and the information technology field (Wikipedia, 2023).

Concurrent engineering is based on two concepts:

1) Including all phases of a product's lifecycle into the planning base already in the early stages of product development

2) different activities occur simultaneously. The target of this latter point is to discover potential flaws in design early in the development process, making fixing the issues less costly and less time consuming than in the case of a waterfall approach to the new product development.

Successful concurrent engineering includes establishing user requirements, creating early design concepts, computer simulations, prototype builds, and eventually manufacturing the final product. By utilizing simultaneous engineering, companies aim to respond to challenges that include:

➢ ever more demanding customers

➢ rapid technological changes

➢ environmental challenges

➢ competitive pressures concerning quality and cost and

➢ shorter time to market with additional features in the complete product (Syan & Menon, 1994).

There are several targets to Simultaneous Engineering. It is utilized in an aim to:

➢ decrease the duration of product development process

➢ improve profitability

➢ increase competitiveness

➢ gain more control over design and manufacturing costs

➢ achieve closer integration between departments

➢ improve the reputation of the company and its products

➢ enhance product quality and

➢ promote team spirit (Syan & Menon, 1994).

9.7.2 Organisational benefits from well-executed concurrent engineering

Just like successful TCO work, the successful development of a complex new product requires a lot of cross-functional collaboration. This also helps to optimise the Total Cost of Ownership of the whole product both for the company that manufactures it, for the direct customer and for end users, in case the latter two differ from each other. Already the collaboration between product development and manufacturing departments can yield significant benefits in multiple aspects, but the benefits materialise even further when more departments are involved in the Concurrent Engineering work, such as supply chain management, maintenance and prototyping (author's experience).

Since concurrent engineering requires a lot of cross-functional teamwork, it brings people from different functions together to achieve a common goal. This can easily lead to improved information flow, collaboration and communication within and between the teams, leading to more effective decision-making.

Secondly, when people from different departments work together, they often come up with ideas that they couldn't have come up with working in their usual teams (Oboloo, 2023). Thanks to this cross-functional teamwork, the silo effect is also further reduced, because the members of different line organisation functions, who would not otherwise end up working together, strive to achieve common goals. In doing so they also gain knowledge and understanding of work outside their own expertise (Meadows Analysis & Design, 2018). This equips these people to implement new and different solutions in their own field of work, too. Furthermore, the manufacturing engineering team gets an early insight into the product, which makes it easier to start engineering the production process around the product. This reduces the effort needed to set up the production process. Additionally, being allowed to participate in Simultaneous Engineering also works as job rotation and gives the feeling of job enrichment, both of which are known to increase motivation. Moreover, job enrichment can improve an organisation's financial performance and labour productivity, reduce absenteeism and turnover, and improve quality output via increased employee satisfaction (Robbins & Judge, 2022, pp. 150-151). And this brings us to the final section of this chapter: Simultaneous Engineering and TCO.

9.7.3 SE & TCO – Mutual benefits

At this point, this might be a very obvious statement: Successful simultaneous engineering yields a multitude of TCO benefits in several aspects. The organisational benefits explained in the previous section all add up to the TCO of the working organisation working in the project, as explained to some extent in the chapter 8. One of the key organisational benefits of successful SE work is the reduced silo, benefitting all people in it through more fluent collaboration and reduced frustration stemming from not being able to understand the expertise background of people from other departments, and the whole company financially thanks to more fluent collaboration which means fewer working hours wasted.

Many other benefits are of the more economical aspect:

- more cost-effective design solutions, saving money from the Total Cost of Ownership of the entire product

- time to market is reduced leading to competitive advantage

- the design flaws can be corrected early, thus leading to less money and effort wasted on multiple revisions on the part (Wikipedia, 2023)

- reduced rework in production and design through more considerations of manufacturing techniques already in the new product development

- reduced throughput time of the product in the production process, leading to improved production capacity

    o or, alternatively, reduced investment or production personnel needs in the production process to achieve the required production capacity

- improved product quality in the production process thanks to the product design that is better suited for the intended manufacturing process

- remarkable cost reductions in the supply chain management when logistics, packaging and key suppliers are all considered in the product design

- improved product quality potentially leading to a competitive edge over competitors' products in the same market segment

- improved customer satisfaction through enhanced product quality and easier aftermarket maintenance of the product if this aspect is considered in the design, often leading to increased revenue and reduced TCO of the product to the end user (author's experience).

Besides the benefits that successful Concurrent Engineering brings to the Total Cost of Ownership of the product to the manufacturer, there are also benefits going to the other way. The principles of TCO can be utilised to justify the seemingly more expensive design solutions.

For example, an additional strengthening beam in the body of the car might be required if the crash test simulations show that the target results of the actual crash test might not be reached without the strengthening beam. There might be a temptation to try to save costs by not adding this part, but it is cheaper to do the work properly on the first time rather than first resisting the advice to add the part, then failing the crash test, risking delays in the project schedule and definitely increasing the total costs by having to do the crash tests multiple times. Let alone all the additional process modification work needed to add the part into the process flow.

TCO can also be utilised when arguing why certain tests should be carried out to make sure the product is being developed in the correct direction. Even though testing is never done for free, going back later to the drawing board to a much earlier phase of the product development process can very easily cost several times more than what it would have cost to do the tests and fix the potential issues immediately.

And perhaps most importantly from Concurrent Engineering point of view, TCO can also be utilised to reason out why concurrent engineering should be included in a complex NPD project. As all these benefits of SE show, neglecting the whole SE phase in such a project pretty much equals asking for trouble in product quality, increased manufacturing costs, increased quantity of product iterations reaching the manufacturing phase, risking delays in the project schedule and worsened financial results in the whole organisation (author's experience).

10   MANUFACTURING AND TCO

TCO has a multitude of application potentials in the environment of industrial manufacturing processes, both during planning and setting up the production process and while running the existing production process. The increasing complexity of the production process and the organisational structure in the company brings additional elements to consider in this context of TCO, too.

In this chapter we shall focus on the industrial manufacturing process and some very foundational TCO elements in it, as well as some methods of optimising the TCO of a manufacturing process. Once again, one keyword is waste. Eliminating waste in processes is one of the certain ways to improve the overall TCO as long as it is done while avoiding adding workload elsewhere in the organisation even more. So, let's get going, starting with one of the key pairs of terms in this context: value-adding work and non-value adding work.

10.1   Value adding and non-value adding work

Value-added (VA) activities are the activities that enhance the product or service, making it worth more or more desirable to the customers. On the other hand, Non-Value-Added (NVA) activities take time, resources, or space, but do not increase the value of the product. Identifying and minimizing Non-Value-Added activities while improving and developing value-added ones is crucial for increasing efficiency, reducing waste, and improving overall customer satisfaction (Marcetic, 2022). Value-adding work includes all the work phases that increase the added value of the service or product ordered by the customer. These include, e.g. casting of the product, painting and assembly. Ultimately, the customer is willing to pay only for the added value of the product (The Finnish Industrial Union, 2020, p. 9), which is why it is important to understand these topics. Even though it is quite a simplification, optimising the TCO of a manufacturing process is quite the same as maximising the share of value-adding work in the total amount of work in the working process. Kaizen is one very effective concept of incremental continuous improvement, which I personally highly recommend following in the search to eliminate waste and non-value adding work in the manufacturing process (author's experience).

A typical workday in a manufacturing company contains also work phases that are necessary to manufacture the product, but don't increase the added value of the end product. These include, for example:

➢ quality checks

➢ handling of the product or its components and assemblies

➢ transferring or transporting materials

➢ time spent preparing the work phases and

➢ assisting work that does not directly prepare for the value adding work but has to be done to be able to resume with value-adding work phases.

Besides these routine work phases, often workdays also contain interference time that includes technical errors and malfunctions, waiting time and searching for parts or tools. Some methods of maximising the share of value-adding work include:

➢ removing unnecessary material transfer and transportation

➢ completing the work phases correctly on the first time

➢ minimising disruptions caused by material and component shortages

➢ minimising the amount of time required to position the parts correctly

➢ minimising preparation work

➢ eliminating unnecessary breaks from work

➢ improving the orderly arrangement of workplaces along the production line

➢ ensuring the readiness to complete work tasks and

➢ facilitating productive work through purposeful processes (The Finnish Industrial Union, 2020, p. 9).

These principles don't apply only to manual work done by us humans, but also to automated work done utilising industrial robots. For example, if the utilisation of different robots in the production line is very unbalanced and this results in unbalanced process completion times in different production cells, the slowest production cells become bottlenecks of the process. But let's move on to the next section to discuss these highly interesting topics further.

10.2   Manufacturing Engineering & Process Engineering and TCO

After product development and simultaneous engineering, we move downstream in the product lifecycle concerning the functions directly in touch with the product itself and lower our anchor to stop at manufacturing engineering and one further, process engineering. There are multiple TCO implications both on their own and together. And even more so when the same personnel have worked in the SE phase concerning the same product. But let's start with manufacturing engineering.

10.2.1   Manufacturing Engineering and TCO

The duties of the Manufacturing Engineering department include lots of different topics related to planning and setting up a production process, as well as commissioning the process equipment and ramping up the production in the newly built production process. There are basically two kinds of project setups with carryover of the equipment: greenfield and brownfield. Brownfield means a production process that is established in the place of the previous production process designed for a different product, including both brand new equipment, and utilization of the existing equipment from the previous production process in an existing facility. Greenfield means utilizing brand new equipment in a facility without any process equipment previously installed in the same location nor any carryover equipment available (author's experience). Completing these projects requires the project personnel to take care of an enormous variety of different duties, such as:

➢ evaluation and development of manufacturing processes

➢ studying equipment requirements, investigating testing methods and collaborating with suppliers

➢ improving manufacturing efficiency through optimization of process flows, space requirements and process layouts

➢ calculating different cost elements for decision-making

➢ collection, analysis and summarization of data and trends when preparing reports

➢ ensuring the process complies with relevant legislation

➢ managing relationships with relevant stakeholders

➢ maintaining product and process databases

➢ keeping up with the technical and professional knowledge (Malsam, 2023).

Manufacturing Engineering projects have a multitude of TCO implications worth a one whole book, but I'll try to summarize them more efficiently here in this section, focusing on the main points both in technical and organizational aspects, trying to bring in more of my experience of 8,5 years in project work so far. I have chosen this approach to avoid just copying or referring to general guidelines existing online, but I shall encourage looking those up at each of the related points. So, let's kick off with the organisational side.

A project starts with a kickoff. The kick-off shares many principles with any project meeting, but also differs from general project meetings in many aspects, too. Because of the similarities, I strongly encourage you, dear reader of this book, to look up the instructions of efficient meeting routines online if you're not already familiar with the topic. However, especially in the topic of the project kick-off, the approach "less is more" might do more damage than good. After all, the kick-off is not only about the product, but the project itself should be the focus. This means that aside from the introduction of the product, targeted production volumes and the tact time the production volume requires, also topics such as project plan, quotation content, project main schedule, stakeholder management, communication plan and project budget must be elaborated in the kick-off, too. Moreover, the kick-off not only elaborates the scope of the project and the work done for it prior to project start, it also sets a tone to the early stages of the project. If the approach to the kick-off "let's get it over with quickly so we can get to work", this approach might spread into project itself and occur, for example, as a rushed preparation of technical specification documentation that then requires multiple rework rounds, costing both time and money.

Secondly, especially a complex industrial project, and basically any project requires a project plan. There are a lot of guidelines available online about how to create a project plan, so we shall not focus on that aspect here. Instead, there is another equally important point to the project plan: making sure it's internalised, understood and followed by the project team. This can be promoted by making the project plan simple to follow, as compact as possible while containing all the crucial information, as well as including it as one of the key parts of the project kick-off.

Third highly important TCO point of organisational topics in the project is the primary schedule. When properly constructed, it shows not only the main deadlines of the project and the most important milestones required to complete them, but also contains all relevant tasks required to complete these milestones and shows the correlation between these tasks. The correlation between tasks is especially important to understand, because this helps the teams of different responsibility areas within the project to consider the colleagues in other teams and other sub-projects in decision-making and work scheduling. After all, any team should not proceed with its tasks without aligning the relevant topics with other teams. For example, if the project contains validation of the equipment design through simulation before proceeding to manufacturing, the work of both equipment design team and simulation team needs to be synchronised in such a manner that both are ready to proceed to the next phase in the correct work order.

The fourth main organisational point of Manufacturing Engineering projects, and the last one in this section, is the project personnel and organisation chart, including both relevant project roles and people suitable to fill these roles. There are many approaches to how these roles should be filled concerning the amount of experience, mix of experience backgrounds and so on, but as a general rule I want to give three different pieces of advice:

1) consider all the roles relevant to the success of the project

2) the more complex the project, the more experienced the personnel in the project should be, if such personnel are available for the project

3) no matter what the "line-up" for the project is, no matter how much experience it contains in which fields, poor leadership and poor management can still make things very messy in the project.

Based on my experience, considering these three points will already carry far in the success of the project when it comes to the project organisation.

Moving on to technical aspects, I also introduce what I think are the three topics with the biggest TCO effects. First one is the technical purchase process in projects. Even though the often-tight schedule in projects creates pressure to "get a move on" with the procurement, creating thorough technical specifications on the first go instead of multiple revisions is actually faster. And not only during the procurement process but also later in the project and during production to fix the faults caused by flawed technical specifications, in the worst case leading to severe technical defects requiring lots of rework, repairing and even scrapping. And scrapping can be an enormous cost during production ramp-up and running the production after the project has been completed. Which is why considering all stakeholders is really important at every phase of the project.

The second technical aspect is the correct level of engineering in the equipment. By this, I want to emphasize the cost effect of over-engineering. Not only does over-engineered equipment cost more to manufacture, but it also costs more in maintenance due to increased complexity and possibly more in process utilities, too. Additionally, more components and moving parts mean more chances of breakdowns, leading to production stoppages, causing downtime and related expenses described in Section 1.3.4.

The third important point I want to highlight is the balance between technical competence and price by suppliers. Supplier selection is often a complex topic in its own right, consisting of supplier mapping and contacting the supplier, creating the technical specifications and discussing them with the supplier candidates. Once this is done, the suppliers submit their quotations, which then must be evaluated to ensure the quotations match what has been asked for and that they fulfil all relevant requirements. Once this has been done, it's time for the supplier selection. This can be done based on multiple criteria, but typically it's based on the technical know-how of the supplier candidates, on previous experiences concerning the collaboration with them and on the initial quotation. As discussed in Section 1.3.1, the initial quotation often forms only 10% of the total life cycle cost of the equipment, which means alone it is insufficient to cover the financial basis of decision making. Moreover, the whole decision is sometimes made based solely on the initial quotation, skipping all other considerations. Personally, I find this a dangerous path to take, especially if the pricing is based on hourly rate times estimated total working hours and the invoicing then happens based on the actualised working hours. This can very easily lead to a situation where the cost of the work done by the supplier greatly exceeds the quotation numbers, while also requiring lots of working hours for evaluation of the work, making correction remarks, having the supplier do their rework and then evaluating it again, even in multiple cycles, repeatedly. This can easily lead to a situation where the supplier that was initially thought to be the cheapest turns out to be the most expensive one when all costs are considered. And if this supplier is, for example, an equipment engineering company and the manufacturing is then done by another company, poor design can lead to increased manufacturing, operation, maintenance, downtime and production costs, as well as reduced remaining value in the means of carrying the equipment over to the next project.

10.2.2   Process Engineering and TCO

Process engineering differs somewhat from manufacturing engineering. Sometimes these two names mean the same in different companies, but there are also companies in which there are both Manufacturing Engineering and Process Engineering departments, in which case Process Engineering focuses more on the existing production and Manufacturing Engineering on designing and setting up new production lines (author's experience). Some duties of a process engineer include:

> ➢ testing, monitoring and maintaining equipment, including conducting regular tests to ensure the equipment complies with prescribed standards

- researching, pricing and collaboration with procurement department when it comes to purchasing new equipment
- designing new equipment as required or redesigning the process flow
- designing, altering and monitoring processes to guarantee maximum output with minimum defects in the production line
- overseeing the plant operations
- ensuring the occupational health and safety
- creating, maintaining and managing the required documentation to comply with safety protocols
- gathering and analysing data about efficiency and budgets to report to management
- analysing every detail and step in the production process flow to reduce costs, enhance productivity and, in general, optimise the production process.
- Analysing every detail and step of the production process to cut costs, increase productivity and optimise the production line (Indeed Editorial Team, 2024).

When the process engineers are responsible for all these topics in an existing manufacturing process, they have a lot to take care of as their routine work. This means that in big companies one process engineer is nowhere near sufficient, unless the chosen strategy is not to develop the process almost at all once the production line has been set up. Since the tasks of process engineers include both monitoring and improving the efficiency of an existing manufacturing process, understanding the thought work behind TCO is highly useful also in this profession. After all, to improve efficiency and save costs in the big picture, it is essential to understand how each change in the process affects both the immediate surrounding process and the entire production chain. Only then we can understand how the changes designed to improve the efficiency of the targeted process area affect the entire production chain. This defines if the planned improvement ends up being an improvement in the big picture in capacity, quality or costs (author's experience).

One such case could be the repacking of the arriving components. If the rack in which the components arrive is not suitable for the type of operation at the station where it's meant to be located, repacking could be an option. This would save costs, for example, in the reduced number of sick leaves by workers at a manual station, thanks to the improved ergonomics. However, when speaking strictly in money, this needs to be weighed against the increased costs of repacking. The new rack needs to be at least as cost-efficient to be handled by the internal logistics as the one currently in use. Depending on the complexity, there can be some other direct cost elements to be considered as well, but usually the consideration ends at direct costs (author's experience). What is often forgotten, or neglected, is the positive psychological effect of ergonomical improvements. One of the standard definitions of good ergonomics is "fitting the work to the worker" concerning both physical and mental demands of the work. Good ergonomics has been proven to benefit the profitability and employee retention, as well as supporting fulfilling the psychological needs as described Section 8.2 (Veena, 2019).

Understanding the principles of product quality is necessary for success in this role, too. After all, we must understand how quality requirements differ in different parts of the product before we can implement any changes to, for example, cut costs in the production process without endangering the end product quality. This requires not "only" understanding the quality requirements in different parts of the product, but also understanding the order in which the product will be assembled. For example, the surface quality requirements in the parts remaining visible in the end product are often different compared to parts that won't remain visible.

10.3 Manufacturing process and TCO

An existing manufacturing process often contains a multitude of TCO implications; we could generalise a bit, stating that the more complex the manufacturing process is and the more internal stakeholders it involves, the more cost elements there are to be factored into the Total Cost of Ownership of the whole manufacturing process.

However, I want to point out one of the key concepts related to manufacturing process terminology and one of the key concepts in investigating all the different phases of an existing manufacturing process and planning how to improve them. The first one concerns the process output, and the second one, enhancing the manufacturing process, concerns work study (author's experience).

10.3.1   Process throughput and TCO

"Throughput is the quantity of a service or product a company can produce over a certain period." (Hayes, 2024). However, when defining the net throughput instead of theoretical capacity of the process, meaning the actual quantity of products that are produced over a certain period, we must also consider the overall equipment effectiveness, OEE (Worximity, 2024). By doing this, we get the real-world total capacity of the process, considering process availability and performance, as well as total quality output of the process. Availability includes planned and unplanned production stoppages during the planned production time, meaning how big percentage of the planned production time the process equipment is operational on average. Performance is related to the running speed of the production, being affected by the slow cycles and small stops, while quality is concerned with defects compared to quality requirements (OEE, 2024). OEE is calculated using the formula $OEE = Technical\ availability\ x\ Performance\ x\ Quality$. For example, if the availability is 96%, performance 97% and quality output 98%, we get the total OEE of 91,2%.

And why is this meaningful in the context of Total Cost of Ownership? When designing and setting up a production line, the net target capacity is one of the key elements of the design basis. After all, different types of equipment can be operated at different speeds. If the process is designed so that only the theoretical capacity, without considering OEE, just barely reaches the targeted production volumes, the OEE must be 100%. In practice, this is not possible in any of the areas of OEE. Reaching 100% OEE would mean having to reach 100% in all three aspects: availability, performance and quality. However, there is no such thing as a production process in which there never are planned or unplanned production stoppages. Comparably, any production process of even moderate complexity contains slow cycles and small stops, because the total cycle time is never the same from station to station. The cycle time can be generalised for the entire process by calculating it from the process output, but practically the work phases at each station are completed in different durations of time. And in practice, quality cannot be a consistent 100% even in a fully automated process, even after having honed all the process parameters to absolute perfection. And one reason behind this is that much of the mechanical components of the automated equipment wear out little by little throughout their operating life. Another reason is tolerances and tolerance chains of the equipment. If the whole tolerance chain of the equipment in one work phase just barely stays within the limits of the quality specifications, any source of inaccuracy might easily cause a defect.

10.3.2   Work study and TCO

The major goal of work study is to improve the productivity, job-wellbeing, and profitability while using safe, effective and economical working methods in a safe, effective and economical working environment (The Finnish Industrial Union, 2020, p. 4). And "despite" its goals, work study brings benefits to the workers, too, through improvement of working methods, improved occupational health and safety and improved continuity of work (The Finnish Industrial Union,

2020, p. 4). Aside from these, successful work study and related process improvements can also add to the income of the workers slightly through production bonuses (author's experience). More general increases in profitability tend to benefit mostly only the owners of the company, unfortunately (author's view).

Just like TCO and life in general, successful work study, and especially the following process development work, requires collaboration. When the employees working on the studied workstations get to participate in the development work by giving ideas and feedback, it enhances their job motivation and job engagement. This also makes it easier to perform the studies required before the development work, because the employees feel this is done for their own benefit, rather than just benefitting their employer at their own expense.

The methods of work study include:

➢ observational study

➢ clocked study

➢ movement time study

➢ working time calculations

➢ standard time systems (The Finnish Industrial Union, 2020, p. 24).

Because work study aims to reduce waste in the working processes while retaining or even improving the occupational safety and, at the same time, productivity of the work, it could be called a "highly TCO-minded method". After all, it is only beneficial to the overall TCO of the complete production process if the waste in processes is reduced. Let's make a quick example calculation: The operator needs to walk 50 steps during each full tact of the station. There are 170 products made per shift, which means 170 tacts per station. In work study, the normal working pace is compared to the walking pace of 4 km/h (=1,11 m/s) and the average length of a human step is 70 cm (Physiopedia, 2024). Through the work study, 50 steps is reduced to 38 steps. How much time is saved per shift?

1) 50 steps – 38 steps = 12 steps. Let's calculate how much time these 12 steps take:

   a. Total length saved: 12 steps x 0,7 m/step = 8,4 m

   b. Time saved: $\dfrac{8,4\ m}{1,11\ m/s} = 7,57\ seconds$/tact

   c. Total time saved: 7,57 seconds/tact x 170 tacts = 1 286,9 seconds = Approx. 21,4 minutes per shift.

This saved time can, for example, enable the worker to work at a more moderate working pace if the station has been previously overloaded. Alternatively, it can provide a saving potential when combined with rebalancing of workstations as a result, potentially even enabling reducing the quantity of workstations when similar gains are achieved throughout the production process (author's experience). I highly recommend work study as one of the key methods of improving productivity and profitability in the manufacturing industry, especially in companies where a big share of total costs comes from manufacturing operations.

10.4   Cost-effective manufacturing solutions and TCO

Everybody wants to be cost-effective in their business operations, right? After all, who would be wasteful on purpose? But there are many ways to be cost-effective. When the financial background of the decision-making is based on the lowest initial price, there is a risk that it leads to very high costs of maintenance, production or downtime, for example. Which is why we must keep the total cost of ownership in mind when aiming for cost-effective manufacturing solutions. In this section we focus more on the physical elements of manufacturing; the things we can see when walking by the production line.

One of the key terms in this section is over-engineering, or more like the avoidance of it. Over-engineering can occur in many shapes and forms. For example, we can have a much higher material thickness in our automated process tools than it needs to be, given the general guidelines of strength multipliers for different materials in different use cases. And as we can imagine, this increases the amount of material needed in these process tools, making them more expensive to manufacture (author's experience). But what else are the cost elements related to this case of over-engineering? One is related to the robots in an automated process. Different industrial robots have different levels of payload, which means the total weight they can handle, including both the process tool attached to the robot and the workpiece the tool is handling, if the tool is used to lift the workpiece (Motion Controls Robotics, 2024). When the process tool, such as a gripper, is much heavier than it needs to be, the workpiece weight allowed for the same robot is reduced by exactly the same weight as the difference between the gripper with correct material thickness and gripper with over-engineered material thickness. This might lead to a situation in which we'll need a bigger robot, which will cost more money. And of course, bigger robots are also more expensive to transport, because we can fit fewer robots into the truck both because of their size and weight. Additionally, heavier pieces of equipment require more robust lifting equipment when installing them in place, which also costs extra money. Weight also sets its own requirements for the packaging of the process tooling, the flooring and so on. Additionally, the extra weight of components can increase maintenance costs, because if they are too heavy to be safely lifted by maintenance workers, additional lifting devices are required.

Aside from material thickness, the quantity of unnecessary components is another common example of over-engineering. And this doesn't mean these components wouldn't be used for anything, but there are engineering solutions that could have been replaced with simpler and lower-cost ones while retaining the same functionality and the same quality results in the end product. Again, also this type of over-engineering increases manufacturing costs and weight, which can easily lead to additional costs described in the previous example. But the increased number of components brings additional cost elements. The more there are components to be removed before gaining access to the actual service or repair item, the longer this work will take. And every kind of labour, apart from charity work, has an hourly rate of labour costs, and costs of equipment used to complete these tasks. Additionally, having more components increases equipment complexity, which can lead to an increased risk of production stoppages and downtime. This leads to multiple additional costs in the forms of production delays, issue resolution and rearrangements to catch up with the production targets, potentially requiring overtime work from production workers, and that is never cheap.

Furthermore, over-engineering does not apply only to mechanics but also to automation. And in modern process equipment, these two go hand in hand. Sometimes poor engineering on one side requires over-engineering on the other to meet the product quality requirements. For example, additional limit sensors and related mechanical solutions might be required in the process equipment to ensure the measurement tolerances of the workpiece remain within the limits set by quality requirements (author's experience).

One form of simple and cost-effective manufacturing solutions is Karakuri, a Japanese term that refers to a lean methodology that contains simple mechanical material handling equipment, which utilises gravity and inertia to move the product across the production area or within the stations. Instead of using computers, hydraulics and other expensive solutions, in Karakuri low-cost mechanisms such as springs, levers, gears and pendulums are utilised. And with simplicity come the benefits of low cost of design, installation and commissioning, maintenance and reduced downtime and lowered costs of modification for future products. This simplicity also means that these devices are very simple to maintain. On the other hand, these devices also need to be modifiable for future products and safe and ergonomically good for the operators to use. After all, their purpose is to ease up the work in manual operations of the manufacturing industry in a simple and cost-efficient fashion (Floyd, 2021).

10.5   Continuous improvement and TCO

In business, we must develop different aspects of operations continuously to keep up with our competition. If our product or operations around it become outdated, we won't stand a chance of obtaining any kind of competitive edge over other companies in the same market segment. But improvements cost money, so what could be the solution in these times of an economic downturn? One answer is incremental continuous improvement, also known as Kaizen in Japanese.

"Kaizen is an approach to creating continuous improvement based on the idea that small, ongoing positive changes can reap significant improvements. Typically, it is based on cooperation and commitment and stands in contrast to approaches that use radical or top-down changes to achieve transformation." (Daniel, 2021). These small positive changes here and there all through the production and surrounding operations don't have to cost a lot of money to implement, yet over time remarkable cost savings can be achieved through these changes. The ten core principles of Kaizen are:

➢ Don't make hasty assumptions.

➢ Solve problems proactively.

➢ Don't settle for the current state of things.

➢ Let go of perfectionism and utilize iterative and adaptive change instead.

➢ Look for solutions when you find mistakes.

➢ Create and foster an environment in which everyone feels empowered to contribute.

➢ Don't accept the obvious issue. Instead, ask "why" five times to find the root cause.

➢ Obtain information and opinions from multiple sources.

➢ Use creativity to find low-cost, small improvements.

➢ Never stop improving (Daniel, 2021).

This approach is more about mindset and spreading it all over the organisation instead of enormous development projects, the latter often costing a lot of money. And even though these big development projects in many cases can achieve an excellently short payback period, the senior management might still feel unsure about kicking off these development projects because of an uncertain future direction of the business, the tough financial situation of the company, or both. As pointed out in the section about quality, however, in a working organisation the management commitment is essential when trying to get a philosophy new to an organisation to spread in every part of it. One way to show this commitment is to show appreciation of development work by providing work time allocation for it alongside the daily routine work.

And how is this related to TCO? Through these incremental minor improvements, we can save on costs in all phases of the product lifecycle and the surrounding operations by implementing small positive changes in all aspects. Some examples we have covered already, for example, in Chapter 4 of this book, so let's focus more on the most typical "habitat" of Kaizen work: production operations. An inefficiently arranged workplace often contains multiple sources of waste, such as transport, waiting and motion. For example, if there is a wear part item in the machine that needs to be replaced every 2-3 hours, we should look for a good place where to put the spares of these wear parts near the location where they are needed, such as by the entry door to the production cell, instead of having to fetch them from somewhere else every time they're needed.

Another very positive aspect of the Kaizen approach, and the mindset behind it, is the improvement work done through collaboration. When production line workers get to contribute to concrete development work by giving their input, their job satisfaction and job engagement are very likely to increase. Of course, some people are more eager to give their input than some others, but it is often very beneficial to listen to the input and feedback from the workers who work in the station where the improvements are done. After all, they usually know every detail of their work after having repeated it so many times, which provides a valuable knowledge base for the development work (author's experience). And in my opinion, there is no better way of improving cost-efficiency in one area than the one that increases job satisfaction and job engagement of those working in this area and at the same time does not increase costs in any other area respectively (author's view).

10.6   Warehousing & internal logistics and TCO

Material management is another major aspect of TCO in manufacturing operations. In the manufacturing industry, warehousing means the process of storing goods, while internal logistics is the operation of transferring these goods between different locations within factory premises. Both contain multiple cost elements, some of which are affected by the same aspects as described in the section 10.4; when an item to be stored and brought to the warehouse is bigger and heavier than it would be with a leaner design, it creates waste both in the internal logistics and warehousing. In warehouse this leads to the need for stronger shelves, and in this context, stronger can mean more expensive. And the bigger the items to be stored are, the fewer of them we can store in the same floor area or the same quantity of standard-size shelf slots. Heavier items might also require additional lifting devices and more robust equipment to transfer them, which increases costs further (author's experience).

But there are so many more sources of cost of warehousing and internal logistics than "just" the size and weight of the items to be handled and stored. Another important aspect is the stock size. Almost nothing in business comes completely free, and warehousing is no exception. The bigger the stock, the bigger the warehousing expense. Aside from the warehouse area, we also must pay for the specific conditions in the warehouse. If we need to maintain stable humidity and temperature, we need to invest more in the machinery capable of retaining these, and we also must invest more in the facility itself, because we cannot retain stable humidity and temperature in a tent-like shelter, for example. This means we should avoid over-engineering in storage facilities, too. That said, we must also consider the work health and safety. Workers shifting from the warm factory area to the cold storage must be provided with purposeful workwear to stay warm. And even though this means arranging the warmer clothes and the cabinets, this is much cheaper than constant sick leaves, decreased job satisfaction and increased personnel turnover resulting from poor working conditions, for example (author's view).

The third major effect on total costs in warehousing and internal logistics comes from the material flow. Poorly controlled material flow can cause a variety of extra costs as product defects and confusion between product variants and related mistakes which lead to a situation in which wrong parts have been delivered to the wrong location, causing rework and even scrapping of the products in the process or, even more expensive, when the product is already finished. Furthermore, if the material flow is not controlled thoroughly, we can end up in a situation where we run out of components, which leads to an unplanned production stoppage until more parts arrive. We must also consider the fact that some materials have an expiry date (author's experience). These materials must be handled on the principle of FIFO, first in, first out (Reid, 2023). If not, we might end up having to scrap the material that could have been utilised if following the correct principle of material flow, thus avoiding scrapping costs total of even dozens of thousands of euros. And one more aspect in this context is the revision of the components or finished products. In the manufacturing industry, the quality of the products is typically developed throughout the product life cycle, but usually much of this development happens in the early stages of production. At this point, it is vital to understand what the latest status of each component is, has the quality improved or worsened with adjustments made to the process, and what the quality status of the components that have gone into manufacturing the products. If we fail at managing the material flow in this context, the chances are that we end up installing the components of "older revision" into the product, ending up with worsened quality of the finished product. This might lead to expensive rework or even more expensive scrapping of the partially or fully finished product.

Internal logistics also needs space to transport the goods, such as components of the product, between the production line and workstations. An excellent solution for this is arranging logistics pathways between the production lines. However, there are multiple things to consider, such as:

➢ Width requirement; how wide are the widest items to be transported using this pathway?

➢ Occupational health and safety; do we have people walking along this pathway, too?

➢ Another aspect of occupational health and safety: Do we operate fuel-powered or electric forklifts inside production facilities?

➢ Pre-conditions set by the chosen method of transporting goods within the facility; does the floor have to be completely flat?

➢ Can we use the same equipment to transport goods indoors and outdoors?

10.7   Maintenance and TCO

Even though maintenance is categorised as one of the cost categories in Total Cost of Ownership, and in some companies, senior management still seems to see maintenance as a source of costs instead of as a source of savings, maintenance function plays an important role when it comes to reducing the Total Cost of Ownership of the whole process over its lifetime. After all, a production stoppage of one day can cost much more in total than the total wage costs of one maintenance worker for the whole year. But let's not finish this section here, because there is so much more to this topic than the obvious comparison.

When purchasing new production equipment, it comes with an operating/maintenance manual either combined or separately. The maintenance section contains multiple things, including the service schedule that should include all the timely inspections, adjustments, lubrications and so on, as well as the correct time or operating cycle interval to replace wear parts. If the maintenance operations have been staffed only to respond to the acute need of breakdowns in the production, the maintenance will always be reactive and never preventive. And it is exactly the preventive maintenance where we can gain a big cost saving. Wear items are often relatively simple to replace, and relatively cheap, too, at least compared to the reactive maintenance when the whole machine fails in the lack of maintenance. And if the preventive maintenance is neglected throughout the production line, soon we will need to shut the whole factory down for even multiple weeks before we can continue manufacturing our products. But this is not the purpose of an annual maintenance shutdown, either. Then it's the time to do those pieces of maintenance operations that require longer periods of production stops, as well as the process improvements that require installing new equipment and so on (author's experience).

Even if cutting on the maintenance staffing costs might be lucrative when looking for the opportunities of saving costs, that leads to one of the strongest forms of sub-optimisation between the budgets: Yes, we do save from the maintenance staffing budget, but at the same time we reduce our profitability, which is damaged by the frequent unplanned production stoppages due to equipment failures. Moreover, these stoppages, as described earlier in this book, require issue resolution work, rearrangements of working time to catch up with the production targets and so on. Equipment failures can also lead to product quality defects, which creates an additional cost of rework and even scrapping, the latter reaching to big sums even per one product in the case of high-complexity products.

What then is a sensible way of saving on maintenance costs without taking a risk of having long periods of downtime? Some of the principles described in the chapter 4 of this book can be applied to maintenance, too, as well as two other points already described: value engineering and avoidance of over-engineering. In the case of maintenance of an existing piece of equipment, value engineering can be summarised as follows: When required, can the components be replaced with cheaper alternatives while retaining their functionality, durability and desired quality level? On the other hand, both aspects are mostly affected already in the product development phase of the piece of machinery in question. When successfully simplifying the design and defining only sufficient materials and material thicknesses, the replacement component cost can be reduced. At the same time, this works as one of the many examples to back up the claim that "cost-efficiency is designed into a product", in other words it's the product development phase where the greatest cost savings can be yielded with smart design choices. The maintenance costs can be greatly reduced through product design solutions.

10.8   TCO and importance of understanding the whole production chain

And now we come to one of the most important aspects of TCO optimisation in the manufacturing operations: understanding how a change in one area of the entire production chain affects another one. The primary target of TCO optimisation is to improve the profitability, and we cannot possibly achieve that if we save in one area while increasing the costs in another area by more than what we just saved as a result.

Let's start with an imaginary example case: The press shop sends the R&D department a request to modify the design of one sheet metal part in such a manner that it is easier and thus cheaper to manufacture. The R&D department then starts the analysis of the request and discovers that the requested alteration takes away one of the guiding surfaces that is important at mounting some other parts and also important to the quality of the final product, which is why the R&D department declines this change proposal. Had this full end-to-end analysis not been made, it would have resulted in quality defects, rework and scrapping, all of which would have cost more than 10 times the amount of euros that the press shop had initially estimated as a saving.

Another example: In order to reach the savings target, the production director decides to cut down on the product finishing, especially in the surface quality checks and related rework criteria. This helps the production director to achieve his or her target of cost savings for the year. At first, it seems that everything is OK, because the final product quality doesn't suffer so badly that it would show in the final inspection of the product within the factory premises. However, soon after the product is launched to the market, the company receives a lot of customer complaints and even claims, because the paint is coming off in exactly those areas where these cost-cutting measures where implemented, which is why the company is forced to issue a product recall. In this recall campaign, all the paint from affected areas is removed, the surface quality is checked and reworked to a better level and then repainted by a professional, costing several thousand euros per product, roughly 500 times as much per product as the production director was thinking to save.

And these examples are why I'm personally not an advocate for siloed thinking in production operations, just like not in any other aspect of business, either. And speaking of organisational silos, TCO work has great potential to reduce the appearance of silo effect between production departments. When tasked with coming up with ways of cost savings together, experts from different departments can come up with solutions that serve all the departments so that the actual total costs are reduced instead of just reallocating the cost into somewhere else within the production chain. In this way, everybody wins; the employees involved feel motivated by the results, and the company can increase its profitability by successfully reducing the total costs while retaining the already competitive selling price of the product (author's experience).

11 SUPPLY CHAIN MANAGEMENT AND TCO

"Supply chain management (SCM) is the monitoring and optimization of the production and distribution of a company's products and services. It seeks to improve and make more efficient all processes involved in turning raw materials and components into final products and getting them to the ultimate customer" (Fernando, 2024). Supply chains are getting more and more complex, which means the transactions don't happen only between the buyer and seller, but there might also be a buyer and a seller, possibly also third and fourth party, who can be service providers, retailers and so on (Caniato et al., 2014). And this is why the total cost analysis is considered one cornerstone of supply chain management (Oskarsson, 2019).

In this chapter, we shall focus on those aspects of supply chain management that are not covered elsewhere within this book, namely focusing on supplier management, supplier contracts, inbound/outbound logistics, packaging and incoming quality control. Somewhat different functions can sometimes manage some of these activities depending on the company. There are several aspects to the Total Cost of Ownership in SCM described aside from the initial price:

- ➢ Transportation and logistics, including e.g.
    - o Packaging and transportation
    - o Temporary warehousing
    - o Duties and taxes + insurance
- ➢ Transaction costs, including e.g.
    - o Search and initiation
    - o Negotiation
    - o Adaptation
- ➢ Financial costs, in other words *capital tie-up* including e.g.
    - o Transportation time
    - o Payment arrangements
    - o Safety stock
- ➢ Risk costs
    - o Quality
    - o Delivery and reputation
    - o Flexibility (Schönsleben, Year unknown).

SCM, being a complex entity, also contains several benefits gained from TCO Analysis:

1) "Better decision making

2) Improved Supply Chain Performance

3) Enhanced Risk Management

4) Improved Supplier Relationship Management

5) Better Inventory Management" (Sunny, 2023).

11.1   Supplier Management and TCO

Supplier management is often referred to as SRM, Supplier Relationship Management, and it aims to ensure the suppliers meet the supply needs of a company effectively, reliably and cost-efficiently. This is done by identifying, evaluating and developing relationships with the suppliers. When executed well, it provides the company a good chance of being successful. In practice, this means supplier negotiations and onboarding of the selected supplier or suppliers, relationship and lifecycle management, communication and supplier reviews. The benefits of successful SRM activities include lowered costs, improved quality of products, enhanced supply chain efficiency and enhanced risk management (The Sourcing Co., Year unknown).

I have also experienced this myself at work. Because of the NDA, non-disclosure agreement, I cannot go into the details, but I can still describe my experience on a general level. The complete business of supplier relationship management starts already upon contacting the potential supplier candidates for the first time. After all, a good first impression helps to smoothen out the initial discussions. Aside from this, well-made technical specifications of the required goods and/or services bring clarity to both parties, and reduce the risk of expensive mistakes. Not only this, but well-made technical specifications also show the potential supplier that the possible customer is willing to put effort into getting what he or she is ordering, instead of just scraping up something hastily and expecting the perfect result in the end. The good technical specifications also ensure the supplier's chances of creating a more accurate quotation with higher chances of the final cost becoming closer to the one initially quoted.

When selecting the supplier, fair treatment of different candidates is very important, as well as the transparency of the supplier selection process both internally and externally. This helps the supplier candidates understand why they were or were not selected, and shows them that the potential customer appreciates their effort. Once the suppliers have been selected, it is important to maintain good collaboration and clear, timely and constructive communication at all times. This enables an efficient, productive and cost-effective collaboration between the supplier and the customer. When problems are solved together in a good spirit, focusing on issue resolution instead of the blame game, it builds a strong bond between the two parties. This helps them both solve even complex dilemmas together, because the strong and respectful connection between the two parties makes them push harder for the common good. This shows positively in many aspects of the entire process going into providing the ordered goods or services, such as good delivery accuracy and good quality. Furthermore, the good relationship between the customer and supplier often increases the willingness of both to be flexible for the benefit of the common good, such as in the case of sudden delivery schedule change (author's experience).

But good supplier relationship management includes more than "just" the strong collaborative connection between the supplier and the customer. It also involves the technical side, which sets its own competence requirements to both parties. Besides the obvious need of a supplier who can deliver the required goods or services in the expected timeline and quality level, the customer contacts of the supplier also need to have a good technical understanding of the goods and services being ordered, so that they can provide the supplier with all the relevant company and industry standards, quality requirements and other technical specifications and instructions (author's experience). And with a new supplier, the background check is important, too, just as it is important to understand the pricing structure, delivery schedule and quality standards to which the supplier must adhere. And there are two more aspects to the supplier management: negotiations and constant evaluation of the supplier through the follow-up of the quality and delivery accuracy of the ordered goods and services (Everything Supply Chain, 2024).

Good supplier relations indeed help save money. There are other methods of saving money in supplier management, too. Supplier consolidation, in other words reducing the number of suppliers, can help a company reduce procurement costs, such as administrative, transportation and inventory costs. In addition, lower prices can be achieved through negotiation. Some ways of trying to affect the total pricing and timing of the payments favourably include:

➢ market research to understand the current prices and trends

➢ economies of scale; trying to achieve a lower piece price through a remarkable order volume

➢ negotiating more favourable payment terms

➢ favouring long-term contracts to attain stability and predictability and

> ➤ asking for discounts.

Supplier management can also be streamlined with the help of automated tools to make the related paperwork and official processes more efficient. This includes automated onboarding processes, automated data entries and automated documentation procedures, for example. And further cost savings can be obtained through successful supplier risk management. Not only does this help to save costs directly, but well-executed supplier risk management also helps make the supply chain less susceptible to disruptions and disturbances. And last but not least, advanced technology in many areas, such as engineering, manufacturing, communications and data systems, can also help the company cut costs related to supplier management (Everything Supply Chain, 2024).

11.2 Supplier Contracts and TCO

Agreements made with suppliers contain a lot of aspects of cost effects. Systematic managing of contracts is called vendor contract management. It includes setting clear conditions, evaluating supplier performance, and making sure that both parties comply with what's been agreed. Successful managing of supplier contracts enhances risk management, helps the company save money and strengthens the supplier relations, and helps the company comply with legal and legislation requirements. Furthermore, well-executed supplier contract management helps the company reduce the administrative burden from topics such as contract tracking and dispute resolution and avoid damage to the reputation and image potentially caused by failing to deliver to its customers because of issues in the supply chain.

The process of supplier contract management includes 5 steps:

1. Determining supplier requirements
2. Evaluating and selecting suppliers
3. Negotiating contract terms
4. Introducing and using a contract management system that utilises automation in administrative tasks of contract management
5. Monitoring supplier performance
6. Renewing or terminating the contracts.

Some of the good practices in contract management include standardised contract templates, promoting collaboration with vendors, utilising purpose-built technological solutions and reviewing and updating the contracts regularly (Carvajal, 2023).

Through the systematic process of supplier contract management it is easier to save money in the supply chain, because the systematic approach involves important action points, such as implementation of lessons learned from the previous contracts, considering differences between different cases and how these differences affect the alterations needed in the contract compared to some other cases. For example, a case of building a production line in a company's own premises requires a different kind of contract than building up the line in customer's premises. The practical differences between these two exemplar cases may include topics like utilisation of different technical in-house norms and differences in responsibilities. The customer's actions might have a very different effect on the success of a project done in their facilities compared to a project done in the supplier's facilities, and this must be considered in the contract (author's experience).

How is this related to the Total Cost of Ownership, then? The supplier contracts may be very detailed or very vague. Both kinds of contracts, and everything in between, have their place, and a huge number of aspects affect the suitability of each contract to each case, but contracts should not only protect both parties with a full-on dispute (author's experience). They should also facilitate collaboration for issue resolution (Nysten-Haarala et al., 2024), for example by providing a special pricing in case some products are suddenly needed in bigger volumes or providing the means of alternative planning in case of supply chain disruptions concerning the components required for the products manufactured by the suppliers. Having a clear contractual basis for situations like this brings clarity to all parties, which makes handling such situations more efficient. This helps all parties make alternative arrangements more efficiently, freeing up time and energy from first wondering and figuring out how each contractual party should approach the problematic situation. And of course, aside from the contractual factors, also mutual trust helps a lot in dealing with problematic situations while retaining the mutual effort to reach the common goal (author's experience).

11.3   Inbound/outbound logistics and TCO

Inbound and outbound logistics form another important aspect of the Total Cost of Ownership in supply chain management. "The first stage of inbound logistics is procurement. Inbound logistics include receiving goods, checking, unloading goods and placement in the warehouse," while outbound logistics includes "warehouse picking and packing and outgoing from the loading dock distribution and transportation."(Logistiikan Maailma, 2024). Thus, the inbound logistics means all the steps included starting from the packaging of the goods by the supplier to be shipped out to the customer all the way until the goods have been placed in the customer's warehouse. This phase of the product lifecycle contains a lot of TCO implications, starting already with the supplier contract, because the contracts often contain one of the vital points of responsibilities for the delivery transport: The delivery terms, also known as INCOTERMS (author's experience).

"Incoterms, widely used terms of sale, are a set of 11 internationally recognized rules which define the responsibilities of sellers and buyers. Incoterms specify who is responsible for paying for and managing the shipment, insurance, documentation, customs clearance, and other logistical activities" (International Trade Administration, Year unknown). And these activities, concerning both the seller and the buyer, require effort, suitable data systems or manual data entries, capable personnel, and so on. Additionally, the selected INCOTERMS affects the interpretation of the agreed delivery date. In practice, this means the agreed delivery date might either mean when the goods are ready to be fetched from the supplier's location or when they arrive at the customer's location (author's experience). And it is important to understand this aspect, because the misunderstanding may cause a risk of schedule delay of 1-2 weeks, or even more, which will create further direct and indirect costs. In such a case, the direct costs include the need to reschedule other activities in a project or production, the effort required both for rescheduling and for the catch-up activities, and the corrective actions to make sure the same mistake is not done again. Indirect costs may include added mistakes caused by the added pressure of a tightening schedule and the resulting rework, for example.

Similarly, the same applies to the case of outbound logistics, which is pretty much the same process as the inbound logistics, but in a reverse order and often shipping out the goods to a different destination compared to from where the goods are coming from in the case of inbound logistics. The costs related to shipping, shipping insurance, customs and so on depend on the agreed INCOTERMS. However, even though each Incoterm is standardised in definition, it is always useful to make sure all contractual parties have understood what they mean in practice to full extent. This helps to avoid unpleasant surprises and potential unnecessary conflicts, making the collaboration between the buyer and the seller more fluent in this aspect, too (author's experience). Rachael Sink (Sink, 2017) has also written other excellent points about TCO topics of inbound and outbound logistics, which I encourage reading in case wanting to know more about TCO in logistics operations. These points include port of entry, shipping time, intellectual property, origin and destination, and method of transportation.

11.4   Packaging and TCO

Packaging is another element of the supply chain management. In this section, we shall stick to the context of packaging as one of the areas of Total Cost of Ownership of running a business in the manufacturing industry, not considering the package itself as the primary product. However, even though I have no experience in the packaging industry, I think many of the points presented in this section can be applied in the packaging industry from the customer's point of view.

When supplying goods, such as raw materials and components, to a manufacturing company, the goods must be packed before they can be shipped out. And when transportation of goods is needed frequently and in enormous volumes, it is very sensible to have packaging experts in the organisation, both packaging designers and dedicated and trained personnel to do the packaging. This way, the packaging remains efficient and the goods safe from damage during transportation. However, this probably most obvious cost aspect is not the only one in packaging, far from it. Because in many cases we cannot load the products side by side so close to each other that they touch each other and also fill the cargo space in the vertical direction, we end up "shipping air", too. And minimizing the empty space in the shipments helps to save costs. And in the case of not very tall packages, this calls for stackable goods, which means the goods can be piled up on top of each other as long as they're packed safely. Not all goods are stackable, which must be considered when planning how to load the packages onto the transportation (author's experience).

Another cost aspect of packaging is adapting the packages to the mode of transport, as well as adapting them to whether the material is shipped in both directions, or only one way. If the packaging needs to be returned empty to the location of the supplier, the packaging should be foldable to maximise the transportation capacity to bring the packages back to the supplier with minimal costs. However, in some cases, the packages that were initially used to deliver raw materials or components to the supplier can then be used by the supplier when delivering the finished goods back to their customer. This is the case in some bilateral contracts, where the customer delivers the components to the supplier for the supplier to make the goods ordered by the customer (author's experience).

Changes at the assembly level for the transportation can also affect packaging. If the assembly sequence of a product is altered and some assembly at the point of transportation becomes different, it needs alterations to the packaging, too. For example, sharp corners or inserts in the steel parts, as well as sizeable but thin sheet metal assemblies, may call for special packaging to prevent them from getting damaged during transportation. In some cases, the changes to the assembly might not cause changes in the packaging, but instead, we might fit fewer or more assemblies in the same package than we could do before.

Packaging also concerns other cost aspects. The packaging that is well suited both for its content in transportation and handling in internal logistics means there's less risk of damage to the raw materials and components when being loaded into packages, being transported and when unloaded. If such damage is missed and the defected part ends up in the product, the costs of repair or scrapping often exceed the costs of having suitable packaging. And last but not least, packaging also affects the work health and safety. It is beneficial to avoid having sharp corners, spikes and other health and safety risks on the package surfaces even when being handled with forklifts or other purpose-built machinery, but it is necessary in the cases of packaging that will be handled manually. Another health and safety aspect of packaging, causing expensive sick leaves and work-related physical issues and injuries, is the ergonomic aspect of the packages. If the package is designed for an automated operation, for example, and then the parts are taken manually from it, the chances are that the design of the packaging hasn't accommodated any safety aspects of the packages for manual operations. In practice, this might mean things like:

➢ sharp corners causing a risk of getting cuts and slices

➢ big slots in between the structure of the packages causing a risk of getting tripped on the metal structure of the package

➢ tall sidewalls above which the workers need to bend to get the parts, causing a risk of back injury.

11.5   Incoming quality control and TCO

Incoming Quality Control (IQC) refers to the quality inspection and approval of purchased raw materials, components or products. "When the supplier sends raw materials or components, the quality is inspected by sampling, and finally it is judged whether the batch of products is accepted or rejected" (IPQC, 2022). Incoming quality control is in a very important position in controlling the quality, and thus costs, of manufacturing. After all, no matter how perfectly we hone the manufacturing process, we cannot manufacture even near perfect products if the quality of the incoming material does not meet the requirements. And if the quality defects of incoming material are not detected during IQC, they might end up on the process line. And this means that when the defect is finally spotted, the work required to fix it often costs more than it would have cost to set the defected part aside, report it internally to the supervisor and externally to the supplier, making a reclamation of it and potentially getting a good replacement instead. Of course, fixing the defects is not always possible in the product, which means this one defected part might create the need to scrap the whole product instead. This can cost thousands of euros per single product, even tens of thousands (author's experience). This emphasizes the importance of IQC even further.

IQC is also in a major role in claims towards the component or material suppliers. After all, it is often the IQC team or department that provides the data needed to back up the claims made to suppliers about faulty items being delivered. In such a case, it is important to have the data available about what happened and when, what is the scope of material or component affected and what is the proposal to credit for these defects (author's experience).

The reasons described above are why having an IQC operation is highly important in trying to save on manufacturing costs. In serial production, the single components rarely cost remarkable sums of money, but scrapping a partially completed product might do and scrapping a complete product definitely does. And just like with production stoppages due to equipment failures; if multiple defected components end up in the production process, creating a need for a lot of rework or even a lot of scrapping of partially or fully completed products, it creates a lot of costs in the forms of:

 ➢ issue resolution

 ➢ overtime to catch up with the production targets

 ➢ potential recall campaigns and damage to the reputation of the company, if the defected products end up with the customers or end users (author's experience).

And all this goes to say that even though having an IQC operation might seem like an enormous expense, leaving it out to save in expenses bites back hard.

12 SUPPORT FUNCTIONS AND MANAGEMENT & TCO

And at last, we come to the final leg of our fascinating travel through the ocean of Total Cost of Ownership. Before we can set our anchor to the final port, let's head through the bay of support functions and management.

And why are these aspects an important part of Total Cost of Ownership, too? As discussed at several points in this book, successful TCO work requires successful cross-functional collaboration. And to get the most out of it, we need to understand the role of each function in the TCO work and how the related concepts can help each function save costs without adding them elsewhere. The role of each function in TCO contains both inputs and outputs, both of which are valuable to the overall success.

Different support functions work to support the core business of a company. These include, e.g:

- finance
- procurement
- HR
- production control
- material management
- sales & marketing
- ICT and
- HSE
- facility and construction.

And of course we must not forget about the management, the big influencer in any process and any change in the company. As already stated, and also backed up within this book, without the management commitment we won't be able to spread the change in the organisation successfully. And that is exactly what is required when implementing TCO into the operations of a company for the first time. These departments have something to give and something to get concerning the Total Cost of Ownership, but we shall start with one of the perhaps most obvious ones, the finance department.

12.1 Finance and TCO

As the second letter of the abbreviation TCO, cost, hints out, TCO is very much related to the finance department. The management accounting team or department provides a lot of information required for TCO calculation, either manually or, ideally, utilising automated data systems and the inbuilt data extracts. When the data system has not been configured from the ground up with Total Cost of Ownership in mind, some data needed for thorough TCO calculations might not be available from the system directly but must be obtained by other means, when feasible. These means may include things like measuring the electricity consumption of the process equipment or digging out the information from technical data sheets and digging into service manuals of process tooling to find the wear parts and their replacement intervals and trying to find the prices for these parts from the data system (author's experience).

In an ideal world, if the data systems allow, the finance department can provide information both about direct costs and indirect costs product by product, albeit some of the indirect costs are very difficult to be allocated correctly to a single product. Then we might have to estimate the allocation per product, practically estimating what is the share of the total indirect costs caused by each product in each phase of the value chain. Additionally, finance professionals have a lot of knowledge that can help with achieving success at TCO work in a working organisation. When handling the company finances, the finance professionals have access to all the relevant information concerning different cost elements and cost categories of the company. This information is valuable in understanding how these costs are interconnected.

And lastly, financial KPIs and depreciation are also important TCO points. After all, depreciation of the process equipment affects the remaining value. Furthermore, the finance department can provide information of interest rates, the effects of decision-making concerning the need for additional internal or externa funding and different financial KPIs.

On the other hand, successful TCO work also benefits the finance department. When able to prove that by implementing the Total Cost of Ownership the company can save considerable amounts of money, the management might be more willing to invest in purposeful financial data systems to provide the data tools necessary for the success of TCO work. And even though this is an added cost instead of a direct cost saving, this investment will pay itself back over time as considerable cost savings through proper optimisation of the TCO of single purchases, as well as the TCO of the entire business. Of course, this requires the proper use of these data systems for the purpose they were intended for. It's only natural in business that company owners are looking for a return on their investment. If this investment is wasted through improper use or not being utilised at all, this might affect the willingness of the company owners to invest in other data system development of the similar nature negatively.

12.2   Procurement and TCO

Based on the literature and online sources on the topic, procurement is one of the most typical application areas for TCO, especially in the manufacturing industry. And most probably this is because goods and services purchased form a major share of the expenses of a company, unless the product of the company is services instead of physical goods. Even in such a case, TCO still brings a lot of added value, but most of the sources on the topic seem to focus on the supply chain management, ICT and procurement. And in this section, we shall focus on the latter of these areas. In this book, the naming procurement is chosen to highlight the connection between the entire process and TCO instead of "only" parts of the procurement process, which are sourcing and purchasing (Shuler, 2021). And I also want to point out the procurement department and the procurement process separately. The procurement department or procurement team, often depending on the total size and complexity of the whole organisation and its field of business, is a part of the whole organisation consisting of procurement professionals. The procurement process, on the other hand, is the entire process of obtaining goods and services from suppliers. And unlike the procurement department or team, the procurement process often involves people also from other teams or departments.

As discussed previously in this book, the goal of TCO work is to improve the profitability in business by investigating, evaluating and comparing cost elements beyond the purchase price. Our brains are hard-wired to use automatic, biased and shortcut thinking by default. Psychologist Daniel Kahneman named this type of thinking as "System 1", stating that 'The operations of System 1 are fast, effortless, associative, and often emotionally charged; they're also governed by habit, so they're difficult either to modify or to control' (Lipkin, 2022). This, combined with the tendency of human mind to look for "easy wins" instead of thinking long-term, can easily lead to a situation in which the whole purchase decision making is based on the initial price, and even that is often lacking cost elements from it, potentially leading to a situation where the aim has been to select the cheapest one of the credible options for a supplier, but what resulted was overall the most expensive one. However, by successfully introducing, implementing and maintaining the TCO approach to the procurement process, this whole situation can be turned upside down. And as described in the opening section of this chapter, procurement refers to the entire process, which means it refers to all the key stakeholders, too. After all, success in any major procurement requires a lot of cross-functional teamwork.

That said, the procurement department is one of the key functions in aiming for successful planning, implementation and execution of TCO. After all, experienced procurement engineers are experts in cost elements related to trade between the buyer and seller. Based on their experience, they might also have an excellent understanding of the market price level, which is of great assistance in creating the initial quotation calculations and cost estimates. The procurement department or team also typically has an excellent understanding of what kind of TCO-related information different suppliers can provide. And being one of the major cost drivers in any business where sourced materials and services form a big share of the total costs, the procurement process should be one of the key aspects of the TCO work in any company, regardless of its internal processes. As we discussed in Chapter 4, these processes are also part of the TCO of a company. However, these processes need to be in place before distinct elements within them can be evaluated in TCO (author's experience).

In the procurement department and procurement process, TCO can be applied in many aspects. Make or buy considerations, supplier quotations and supplier selection being just some examples, as well as timing the purchases according to the pricing fluctuations, as discussed in the section 3.7. TCO can also be utilized in supplier negotiations, because aside from helping to guide the discovery and utilization of cost saving potentials, TCO can also aid the negotiation parties at achieving a win-win negotiation result, for example by guiding negotiation about the balance between over-the-table CAPEX payments and their amortization in the piece price. Thus, TCO is, or at least should be, also very important to the procurement team. And the procurement team is also vital to TCO, because by reporting the total savings achieved with TCO work with the assistance of the finance department, it can show the true added value achieved. And, depending on the rewarding methods and criteria in place, the members of the sourcing team might also receive bonus payments depending on how much is saved through TCO work.

12.3   Management and TCO

Management is one of the key stakeholders in any transformational change, also the implementation of TCO in a working organisation. Moreover, management should be very interested in the chance to both increase the profitability of the business and decrease the silo effect in the organisation. On the other hand, management is also in a key position to provide required resources for the implementation of TCO.

When any change process is started in the company, the management is in an important position to boost the success of the change through internal communication, incentives and other methods of boosting the change implementation. By showing how the ongoing change is linked to the vision and mission of the company, and thus also to the strategy, the senior management can engage both middle and lower management, as well as workers, to do their part for the success of the change. Of course, this alone does not guarantee the success, but it helps a lot (author's experience).

The second point is the huge potential for increasing business profitability that TCO has. This should be interesting to the senior management in two ways: firstly, for the benefit of the company and secondly for their own benefit, because profitability is often one of the incentive criteria for the senior management.

Third point, the decreasing of the silo effect, is another benefit for the whole organisation. The success of TCO work requires a lot of cross-functional collaboration, which creates new networks of business relationships within the organisation. This encourages the personnel to look for answers to questions and share information outside their own team or own department (author's experience).

Furthermore, the successful implementation of TCO in a working organisation requires both people and non-human resources, such as ICT and software tools, which can be costly in some cases. Usually, the decisions concerning the effort put into internal development projects and major investments done for them are made by the senior management. In a big organisation with several organisational functions and multiple products being manufactured and developed, Total Cost of Ownership is a complex topic to map out. This complex work requires a lot of time and dedicated personnel to take care of it, as well as reliable software tools to ensure the success of the work.

Lastly, there is one more major benefit besides profitability, the improvement in the quality of financial decision making that the top management can get through TCO; when the financial information concerning a purchase decision is based on the estimated total expenditure over the asset lifetime instead of just the purchase price, the management can make decisions more safely and trust that the selected option stands a good chance of bringing in more profit.

12.4   HR and TCO

As already discussed within this book, for example in Section 2.8, the incentive system is one of the elements in reducing the silo effect. The silo effect is harmful to organizational performance because of the focus on narrow private objectives and causing organizational fragmentation. This can be tackled, e.g. through competence management, which is one of the expertise areas of HR functions. For example, HR can encourage creating and fostering communities of practice, groups of experts from different functions working together to achieve common goals. These communities of practice, CoP's, can be utilised to ease up the transfer of knowledge. However, HR can also be susceptible to the silo effect. To tackle this phenomenon, exposing the HR professionals to cross-functional collaboration is beneficial (Forsten-Astikainen, 2017).

Another way for HR to try to reduce the silo effect is the purposeful incentive strategy based on mutual collaboration instead of rewarding individual performance over the success of the entire organization. For example, in a major project, the profitability-based bonus criteria should at least concern the financial result of the entire project, but preferably the financial result of the whole organisation. If the individualistic bonus target of financial performance is combined with certain features of human nature, such as the tendency for decisiveness instead of engaging subordinates and willingness to use the position of power, the results can be very destructive for the performance of the organisation (author's experience).

On the other hand, just like any department, HR can also benefit from successful TCO work in return on invest (ROI) and payback period calculations. For example, if the HR director sees that a new Human Resource Management System is required due to the greatly increased size of the organisation, procuring, implementing, training and using such a system can be justified through ROI calculations based on the Total Cost of Ownership.

12.5   Production Control & Material Management and TCO

The production control and material management departments or teams play an important role in the overall total cost of ownership of running a manufacturing business, too. Of course, in small companies these might be assigned to certain individuals alongside other tasks or there might be one dedicated person taking care of these functions. Whichever the arrangement, these functions are also required for the successful manufacturing operations, but they're often forgotten in the decision-making within the teams more immediately in touch with the production line when these two functions are not represented in the decision-making forum (author's experience).

Production Control, also known as Production Planning and Control, is responsible for production scheduling either based on in-house information or, especially in the case of contract manufacturing, based on the product orders from the customer. In some cases, the responsibilities of this department also include ensuring maximising the use of available production capacity considering the available personnel, tools and equipment. Tasks like capacity planning, shop order releases, dispatch scheduling and coordinating the requirements concerning the materials and labour needed to finish the product according to its technical specifications are a part of the work scope of Production Control (University of Michigan, 2024). From the TCO point of view, the collaboration and information exchange with the Production Control department is valuable, because this department has first-hand knowledge about the required production schedule of the product based on the customer orders. During industrialisation projects, this helps the project team plan the activities accordingly for all project phases, because the timing of many project milestones is based on the production schedule, mostly concerning four topics about it:

1. Start of Production date for serial products, SoP

2. Date to start manufacturing the first pre-production examples

3. Ramp-up curve, meaning how steeply the production volume needs to be increased from point 2 to point 1

4. Timing and production of possible pre-series phases before the start of serial production.

On the other hand, just like many other support functions, Production Control can also benefit from TCO. If the Production Control department is struggling with challenges that could be solved with a more sophisticated ICT system and successful implementation of it, for example, the principles of TCO can be applied in the payback period calculation. In practice, the cost elements involved in this calculation include estimations of additional manual work required without the system, potentially increased risk of human error without a purpose-built ICT system and thus affecting the punctuality of product deliveries to customers and other issues related to both controlling the production volumes and the quality (author's experience).

Material Management function is responsible for:

➢ "collaborating with other managers to determine supply needs

- ➢ purchasing supplies and materials according to specifications
- ➢ coordinating and supervising the receiving and warehousing procedures" (Bika, 2020).

This makes the Material Management function one of the key stakeholders for the project teams responsible for setting up the production line, especially during the production phases prior to and during the start of the serial production, because this function has the best visibility of the production material availability in the stock. During the serial production, material management also upkeeps the information and follows the changes concerning the stocks of material available for manufacturing the products. And to manage these tasks, the Material Management function needs sufficient organisation and non-human resources to manage these tasks. And once again, this is where the TCO steps in for the benefit of this function.

Furthermore, a benefit of successful and strategic TCO work for both functions is that the success at TCO requires involving and engaging these functions early in the project, which means these functions get to give their input and affect the decision-making in a project, giving them the feeling of appreciation, which has a great potential of increasing the organisational performance, as described in the section 8.2.

The important information input by Production Control and Material Management includes things like:

- ➢ production ramp-up curve
- ➢ when should each variant of the product be produced
- ➢ in-house material flow
- ➢ requirements for materials and labour
- ➢ production material availability
- ➢ delivery schedule of production material.

12.6   Internal communications and TCO

The responsibilities of a person, team or department responsible for internal communications include:

- ➢ developing an internal communication strategy
- ➢ managing internal communication channels
- ➢ implementing new internal communication technologies
- ➢ creating and curating content
- ➢ collaboration with other departments, teams or people and

> ➤ tracking and improving staff engagement (Blink, 2023).

And how does the Internal Communications team affect the total cost of ownership of running a business? The fluent flow of internal information provides a solid decision-making basis concerning the things going on in the organisation for the lower and middle management, as well as their subordinates. For example, the clear communication about concrete actions taken to advance the business strategy of the company brings the clarity and the feeling of progress to the personnel, which has a great potential to increase the morale and job engagement of the personnel (author's experience). One of these actions might very well be an internal development project to implement Total Cost of Ownership into daily business operations, for example.

Furthermore, the internal communication channels on social media or applications of internal communication, such as Skype or Microsoft Teams, provide an easy way for people from different departments to communicate together, agree the activities outside working hours together and so on. This benefits the company greatly, because the employees build a network of relationships outside their own team and immediate surrounding organisation, making the cross-functional collaboration more fluent on work topics, too (author's experience).

The benefits of Total Cost of Ownership are very similar to the ones described in the previous section, related to improved stakeholder management and stakeholder engagement, as well as the potential to get enhanced data systems and other tools available thanks to payback period calculations "fortified" with TCO calculations (author's view).

12.7   Sales & marketing and TCO

The sales and marketing function is one of the major internal stakeholders when it comes to the financial result of the company. After all, this function is the major "counter partner" of the potential customer during the commercial negotiations, together with the top management of the company, of course. And even though in the manufacturing industry sales & marketing expenses don't form a big share of total costs of the business in most cases, the quotation phase has a big impact on the budgets of an extensive project, for example. After all, the project budget is usually the same as the sales price minus the profit margin, potential contingency and a possible management reserve. If the potential supplier has to give in a lot in regards with the pricing, the company is often forced to come up with less costly alternatives for initially planned technical solutions, as well as take more financial risk to itself. The latter is the case especially if the potential supplier has already studied the potential alternatives for the technical solution very extensively, come up with the best available solution based on expert opinion and still has to lower the price during the negotiation process. In this case, the risk of budget overrun becomes very high, which reduces the profitability of the company. And even though the income from the commercial agreement concerning, e.g. a major project is not cost, it has an impact on the project costs as well (author experience).

The more unrealistic the project budget ends up being compared to the technical scope of the project, the more additional work with very little value is created. Because when the budget is very tight, the project management might set very tight restrictions on purchase approvals and processes, which requires extra work when thinking of a thorough argumentation to why some purchases outside the original plan should be made. Furthermore, reports concerning budget overruns cause extra workload to relevant professionals, such as project finance functions, managers and the steering group. Since project overrun is often followed up in several forums, another additional expense is the time of attendees consumed going through the topic of financial overrun (author's experience).

Additionally, the sales department is responsible for the commercial terms with the customer, and handover from the sales phase to the project team or manufacturing organisation. This is crucial to ensure the information from the sales phase downstream to later phases, so planning and execution can be done as agreed with the customer. This way, the whole organisation can be more certain that the resulting product will adhere to what has been agreed with the customer (author's experience). Besides this, Sales and Marketing has important expertise of TCO elements of the entire company from the sales phase and marketing operations.

How then can the sales and marketing function utilise TCO frameworks? With TCO, the seller can measure, document and communicate the value the offering of the company provides for the customer through the lowest total lifetime costs compared to the competition. The TCO analysis can provide a powerful selling point, but it requires experts from both the buyer and seller organisation to work closely together to map and construct the relevant TCO model for the target customer. This process can strengthen the long-term buyer-seller relationship between the two organisations (Piscopo et al., 2008). This is the biggest TCO benefit unique to sales and marketing. Other major benefits are similar to the ones described in previous sections.

12.8   ICT and TCO

ICT function is another major stakeholder in the total cost of ownership of running a business, especially in the modern age. For example, big engineering companies need a lot of software licenses that can cost up to dozens of thousands of euros annually each, let alone major Enterprise Resource Planning (ERP) software and other ICT systems necessary to run a complex business. But even though this software is expensive, it still helps the company save money by saving tons and tons of manual work to take care of the same operations that are partially or fully automated with data systems.

However, these data systems also form one of the major hidden costs of running a business. If a company does not know exactly which additional licenses it might need for a customer project, for example, it tends to either neglect or underestimate the funds needed for the necessary software, thus ending up either not purchasing or renting the needed software or procuring it on its own expense, which has a negative impact on the company profitability (author's experience).

Besides the software and data systems used internally, often major companies utilise data systems to access the same mutual database or data library. This is done to ensure a timely flow of up-to-date data and to make sure all parties stay on track of the product engineering changes, for example. And arranging these mutually utilised data systems and relevant accesses on either side costs time and money (author's experience).

However, ICT systems can also lower the total cost of ownership of running a business. Aside from the example described in the opening paragraph of this section, the ICT software brings a lot of value directly to the TCO work in the form of internal data storing and data sharing systems and, for example, software that helps at should-cost analysis by giving the idea of what a certain product or process equipment design should cost to manufacture, given the present engineering, manufacturing labour and material and other relevant rates. This way, a company can determine if the pricing their suppliers are quoting for them is acceptable based on market values, avoiding paying a premium without added value (author's experience).

Another very visible TCO benefit of ICT is the internal communication and data storing and data sharing systems, as well as Microsoft Office or similar products, for example. Timely information, combined with a lot of different ICT software for different purposes, increases the efficiency and reliability of the work done in a major industrialisation project, for example.

But how does TCO work benefit the ICT department? Just like with any other department, the identification of related hidden costs and the saving potentials in these hidden costs through internal development work and software upgrades can help the ICT department convince the senior management that these things are necessary to improve the productivity and quality of the work, thus increasing the profitability of the business. This applies to both new or improved versions or alternatives of the currently utilised software and to software solutions that haven't been utilised in the company before. With the principles of TCO, it is possible to uncover more hidden costs that contain possibly previously undiscovered saving potentials, further shortening the payback period of the ICT investments while still keeping the calculations truthful.

12.9   HSE and TCO

Health, safety and the environment are a big part of the total cost of ownership of running a business. In fact, we could go as far as calling this topic one of the most important ones in the whole equation of TCO, because it is us humans who manufacture the products manually using tools or design robots and related process equipment for an automated process. And it doesn't have to be either or; a manufacturing process often contains both automated work phases and manual phases. When a robot and a human work on the same workstation, it sets its own unique safety requirements for the manufacturing process (author's experience).

In general, good work health and work safety form a huge factor in any organisation, saving costs both directly and indirectly. One of the major direct cost savings is the savings related to sick leave. Of course, a common cold or other illness is a part of life, but good work safety does definitely reduce the risk of injuries and harmful accidents at work. For example, the purposeful workwear protects the workers from things like sparks damaging the skin and from getting cuts, wounds and eye injuries. Many factors affect the costs, such as the type and severity of the injury, legislation concerning the employer's responsibilities in the event of an incident and so on, but a major injury is never cheap. Because of these factors, there's no one solid truth to how much each accident costs to the company, but one example is given by a study conducted in an exploration and production company, arriving at the average of 14 000 GBP per incident (Hudson & Stephens, 2000). Additionally, crash barriers protect the workers from getting hit by runaway trailers of internal logistics equipment or from potential accidents with very wide items being transported with a forklift, for example. But good work health and safety also decreases the occurrence of common illnesses, because good level of work health and safety creates a safe environment for workers, which reduces the work-related stress experienced by the employees, when compared to an unsafe workplace (Brosschot et al., 2018). This also allows the workers to perform better, which increases productivity, creativity and profitability.

HSE department develops safety management policies, prepares safety reports for the management and investigates workplace incidents (Indeed Editorial Team, 2024) as well as provides expert information concerning workplace health and safety regulations to other internal stakeholders, for example, to process planning and manufacturing engineering departments. This way, these departments can consider safety regulations in their work. The duties of the HSE department include:

- *"maintaining and applying knowledge of the current environment, health, and safety policies, regulations, and industrial processes*
- *reviewing plans and specifications for new machinery and equipment to make sure they meet safety requirements*
- *identifying and correcting potential human and environmental hazards by inspecting facilities, machinery, and safety equipment*
- *evaluating the effectiveness of various industrial control mechanisms*
- *ensuring that facilities and job sites comply with health and safety regulations*
- *guiding the installation and testing of safety guards, devices and interlocks*
- *reviewing employee and environmental safety programs and recommending improvements"* (Office of Energy Efficiency & Renewable Energy, Year unknown).

But health and safety are not the only parts of the scope of work for the HSE department. The natural environment is always affected in some way by conducting business, both directly and indirectly in most cases. The environmental aspect of the HSE function can be summarised as minimising the environmental impact and promoting sustainability. In practice, this means reducing the consumption of resources, generation of waste, damage to ecosystems and pollution as much as possible. This can be achieved through actions such as recycling programs and utilisation of renewable energy sources. And this, too, has both a direct and indirect impact on the Total Cost of Ownership of running a business, because successful utilisation of environmentally friendly practices can minimise the negative impacts on our planet, save costs and enhance the company's reputation in the process (EcoOnline, Year Unknown).

12.10 Facility & construction and TCO

And very last, but definitely not least, the manufacturing process also requires one or more facilities in which to make the product and run the surrounding operations. In the context of the manufacturing industry, we shall focus on the production facility, both the alterations of the existing ones and building new ones. However, we shall not dive deep into the TCO of the construction industry. I'm sure someone more knowledgeable of construction industry can come up with a much better book on the topic than I could.

There are lots and lots of different industrial production facilities. The requirements of the facility depend on many factors, such as the purpose of the facility and requirements set by natural conditions and by the product being produced. For example, some industries apply very strict requirements of product hygiene, general cleanliness, prevention of electric conductivity, humidity or temperature. And this means specific investments in the production facility and warehouses. It is overall still cheaper to build a facility to be fit for the planned purpose rather than first building it very cheaply and then fixing issues and doing the required additional investments and other activities required to make the facility fit for the planned purpose (author's experience).

The technical scope of building a new or altering an existing production facility contains work related to electronics, pneumatics, water supplies, construction work, social spaces and office rooms, as well as HVAC, which stands for Heat, Ventilation and Air Conditioning (Sheldon, Year unknown). And all these fields of work in construction require specialised knowledge to execute them well both in case of constructing a new facility or modifying or renovating an existing one, because with specialised knowledge comes the competence to account for all the aspects, regulations, norms and standards needed to build safe, good and durable facilities (author's experience). After all, if the facility surrounding a production line is poorly built, the inevitable damage to the building in such a situation will create a lot of expenses in the form of both facility repairs and production equipment repairs. Building the facility poorly might also make the effort and money gone into setting up specific production conditions useless. Because what's the value of the investments made to set up required production conditions concerning humidity and temperature, for example, when the roof is leaking, and water is dripping down onto the product? This is why, when needing renovations to existing facilities or needing to build up new ones, a manufacturing company would do wisely if outsourcing the whole scope to professionals, unless there are some, for example, in the facility department. Or, if the company has a lot of this kind of work to be done, it can consider establishing a separate team or even department to take care of these topics (author's experience).

Many areas of business contain a lot of unexpected costs stemming from poor planning and execution, and production facilities are definitely one of them. For example, when moisture gets into the structure of the facility and spreads around, it begins to create moulds. This represents a severe risk of even major issues both to the facility and, most importantly, to the people working inside it (author's experience). Even minor exposure to moulds can trigger symptoms in more sensitive people, while those suffering from conditions like asthma, exposure to moulds can cause wheezing and asthma attacks. Long-term exposure to mould is also known to weaken the immune system even in completely healthy individuals. When the toxicity of mould exposure increases, the people exposed to it can experience persistent headaches and migraines, increased exhaustion and muscle cramps at random. In more severe cases, it can also cause sensitivity to light and unexplained weight gain and hair loss. Aside from physical effects, some cases of prolonged exposure to moulds have also shown to cause insomnia, confusion, difficulty in concentrating, depression, anxiety and loss of appetite (NLR, 2024).

However, often the major tasks of a facility unit focus on the maintenance of the existing facilities instead of building new ones. This includes the production buildings, electrical transformers, existing cooling systems, and so on. And just like production equipment, the surrounding facility benefits from regular maintenance, too. Even though this might feel like an additional expense, regular maintenance is often cheaper than only fixing in a reactive fashion, unless the purpose is to do just the bare minimum to keep the facilities standing up (author's experience).

13 FINAL WORDS, CONCLUSIONS, REFERENCES TO FURTHER RESEARCH

You, dear reader, might have noticed that throughout the book I have several references to oceans and sailing. And this has nothing to do with my personal interests, but with how I see the TCO: an endless ocean that, just when we think we have learned, seen and discovered it all, reveals another aspect of itself. And just like an ocean, it is never the same; there is no single, universally applicable model of TCO that works everywhere. On the contrary, we must identify the "pain points" of the organisation where we can feasibly achieve the biggest cost savings through incremental improvements.

I'm quite convinced that even though the coverage of topics in this book concerning the manufacturing industry is quite extensive, we will still discover more and more ways to utilise Total Cost of Ownership. And, of course, if you want to learn more about any of the topics introduced within this book, You are more than welcome to refer to any of the sources I have listed at the end of this book. And we can find plenty more information online on some topics described in this book. However, at this point I'd like to emphasize the word some because not all the topics introduced in this book seem to have been connected to Total Cost of Ownership in the research nor in online writings on the topic. However, I see TCO as this extensive topic, and more within manufacturing industry alone, and based on what I have read and studied to write this book, TCO is also applied in construction and ICT industries.

As the final words before the credits and words of thanks, I want to say this has been a long but fascinating journey of professional knowledge and growth, taken a lot of effort but still been rewarding. And I highly recommend doing the same for anyone who enjoys writing and has a topic to write about. Speaking of writing, I highly doubt this will be the only book I'll ever write. In fact, I already have ideas for further TCO books, potentially deep-diving some topics introduced in this book and some outside these topics. So, if you have enjoyed this book, I can quite confidently promise that you will get to read more about TCO in the not very distant future. Take care and all the best for your fascinating journey of learning and discovering new things and new knowledge!

Credits and words of thanks

A lot of effort and time have gone into making this book. And now it's time to thank those who have made it possible. After all, life's about much more than writing one book, and the inspiration to complete works like this doesn't come out of thin air. Which is why I'd like to thank:

- ➢ my wife, who has pushed me to grow professionally, who's guided me in a sometimes stern, but supportive fashion and thanks to whom I've taken up pride about my work without being egoistic about it

- ➢ my son, whose growth and development, nearing age 5, keeps on fascinating me and who always brings light to my days

- ➢ my parents, who have taught me many important things about life; far more important than this book

- ➢ my sister, whom I can trust with absolutely everything and who has definitely been one of the key people in inspiring me to strive to put more effort into professional growth

- ➢ my two best friends for their continuous support in my efforts to complete this book

- ➢ Simon Sinek for providing me with inspiration to find my *why* through his works

- ➢ Ville Mäkinen, CEO at iSearch Group Oy, for his words of encouragement and support

- ➢ Lauri Fagerlund, CEO at Lafa Oy, for being an all-round inspiring entrepreneur, also inspiring me to channel my professional knowledge and ways of thinking these professional topics into writing this book

- ➢ anyone who's shown me his or her interest in this topic. It tells me there are people willing to hear more about this fascinating theme.

List of sources of information

➢ Forbes. (2015). *Thoughts on the business of life.* https://www.forbes.com/quotes/5890/

➢ Ellram, L. (1993), Total Cost of Ownership: Elements and Implementation. *International Journal of Purchasing and Materials Management, 29,* 2-11. https://doi.org/10.1111/j.1745-493X.1993.tb00013.x

➢ Law Insider Inc. (2013–2024). *Line Fallout definition.* https://www.lawinsider.com/dictionary/line-fallout

➢ Spencer, L. (29.8.2024). What is Total Cost of Ownership (TCO) in Project Management? *Bricks.* https://www.thebricks.com/resources/what-is-total-cost-of-ownership-tco-in-project-management

➢ Fernandes, T. (29.3.2023). Program Manager's Guide to Prioritization: Strategies for Success. *Medium.* https://medium.com/pm101/program-managers-guide-to-prioritization-strategies-for-success-6d6a1df5d0a8

➢ Logistiikan maailma. (2024). *Total Cost of Ownership – TCO thinking.* https://www.logistiikanmaailma.fi/en/buyingselling/procurement-and-purchases/total-cost-of-ownership-tco-thinking/

➢ Fishman Corporation. (2024). *Manufacturers Increasingly ask Vendors for Total Cost of Ownership Analysis in Addition to Purchase Price.* https://www.fishmancorp.com/tco/

➢ Graco Inc. (2024). *How to calculate total cost of ownership.* https://www.graco.com/us/en/in-plant-manufacturing/solutions/articles/how-to-calculate-total-cost-of-ownership.html

➢ Manutan. (2.6.2022). *What are the components of TCO?* https://www.manutan.com/blog/en/glossary/understanding-tco-total-cost-of-ownership-origins-definition-calculation-advantages-and-so-on

➢ Feldstein, M. & Rotschild, M. (1974). Towards an Economic Theory of Replacement Investment. *Econometrica, 42*(3), 393–424. https://doi.org/10.2307/1911781

➢ Cooper, Z. (6.4.2020). *A practical guide to writing technical specs.* https://stackoverflow.blog/2020/04/06/a-practical-guide-to-writing-technical-specs/

➢ Moody's. (2024). *Supplier risk management.* https://www.moodys.com/web/en/us/supplier-risk.html?cid=ppc-gglds-

17364&gad_source=1&gclid=EAIaIQobChMI1N_L7suwiAMVsUKRBR3KsBGkEAAYASAAEg
J9e_D_BwE&gclsrc=aw.ds

➢ Scholz, K. (Year unknown). *How digital prototypes become hardware in high volume
production.*
https://citeseerx.ist.psu.edu/document?repid=rep1&type=pdf&doi=4fead4dda215ac9a7
04e24e7ea4e2fa309c79973

➢ Technology Industry Employers of Finland. (2024). *Collective agreement employees
between Technology Industry Employers of Finland and Industrial Union, 6 Febuary 2023
– 30 November 2024.*
https://www.teknologiatyonantajat.fi/sites/teknologiatyonantajat/files/inline-
files/Collective%20agreement%202023-2024_www15052023.pdf

➢ Kenton, W. (26.2.2024). Operating Expense (OpEx) Definition and Examples.
Investopedia. https://www.investopedia.com/terms/o/operating_expense.asp

➢ Chen, D., Lee, J., Sleyster, B. & Aunins, T. (2014). *Utility Systems.* Media Wiki.
https://processdesign.mccormick.northwestern.edu/index.php/Utility_systems

➢ ServiceChannel. (2024). *Becoming a Maintenance Worker: Job Description, Skills, and
Responsibilities.* https://servicechannel.com/blog/becoming-a-maintenance-worker/

➢ Six.sigma.us. (2024). *How to do Root Cause Analysis? Everything You Need to Know.*
https://www.6sigma.us/rca/how-to-do-root-cause-analysis/

➢ Yadav, C. (13.3.2023). Cost of Unplanned Downtime in Manufacturing (And How to
Avoid That). *Plutomen.* https://pluto-men.com/cost-of-unplanned-downtime-in-
manufacturing-how-avoid-that/

➢ Tuovila, A. (25.6.2024). Residual Value Explained, With Calculation and Examples.
Investopedia. https://www.investopedia.com/terms/r/residual-value.asp

➢ Cephas, C. (2022). The Math of Manufacturing – How Total Cost of Ownership Impacts
Reshoring Decisions. *Tapecon.* https://www.tapecon.com/blog/the-math-of-
manufacturing-how-total-cost-of-ownership-impacts-reshoring-decisions

➢ Collins, P. & Hull, F. (2002). Early simultaneous influence of manufacturing across stages
of product development process: Impact on time and cost. *International Journal of
Innovation Management,* 6(1), 1–24. https://research-ebsco-

com.proxy.uwasa.fi/c/slwlh3/viewer/html/ivgpaejgbn

➢ Advice-Manufacturing. (2024). *Value Analysis (VA) and Value Engineering (VE): Definitions and Benefits.* http://www.advice-manufacturing.com/Value-Analysis.html

➢ Dell'Isola, A. (1997). *Value Engineering: Practical Applications for Design, Construction & Maintenance Operations.* John Wiley & Sons, Inc. https://books.google.fi/books?hl=en&lr=&id=UzVxDwAAQBAJ&oi=fnd&pg=PR9&dq =info:hxS9qdRUesAJ:scholar.google.com/&ots=y4gkVC89wd&sig=vAeCgdD1isML0R ZNap3OkUkMBUA&redir_esc=y#v=onepage&q&f=false

➢ Reuter, V. (1968). The Success Story of Value Analysis Value Engineering. *Journal of Purchasing, 4*(2), 4–80. https://onlinelibrary.wiley.com/doi/epdf/10.1111/j.1745-493X.1968.tb00088.x

➢ Van der Schans, E., van Lijssel, J.W.N., van Steenderen, P. (2001). Value Analysis: Capturing Total Cost of Ownership reduction opportunities in E&P projects. *Netherlands Journal of Geosciences, 80*(1), 107–111. https://www.cambridge.org/core/services/aop-cambridge-core/content/view/85584D60962FAD4359235B46F4A22323/S0016774600022216a.pdf/ value-analysis-capturing-total-cost-of-ownership-reduction-opportunities-in-eandp-projects.pdf

➢ Lane Davis, K.,E. (2004). Finding Value in the Value Engineering Process: a Publication of the American Association of Cost Engineers. *Cost Engineering, 46*(12), 24-27. https://www.proquest.com/scholarly-journals/finding-value-engineering-process/docview/220449048/se-2

➢ EMyth. (28.3.2022). 6 factors that shape your product's perceived value for your customer. *LinkedIn.* https://www.linkedin.com/pulse/6-factors-shape-your-products-perceived-value-customer-emyth?trk=articles_directory

➢ Macedo, H. (2024). *A practical guide to cost engineering.* Routledge.

➢ IBM. (Year unknown). *What is mean time to repair (MTTR)?* https://www.ibm.com/topics/mttr

➢ Schneider Electric. (19.3.2015). KPI: Mean Cost to Repair (MCTR). *Schneider Electric Blog.* https://blog.se.com/digital-transformation/it-management/2015/03/19/kpi-mean-cost-to-repair-mctr/

➢ Kenton, W. (25.4.2024). Make-or-Buy Decision Explained: How to Make Outsourcing Decisions. *Investopedia.* https://www.investopedia.com/terms/m/make-or-buy-decision.asp

➢ Tilastokeskus. (2024). *Liikevaihto*. https://stat.fi/meta/kas/lvaihto.html

➢ Järvenpää, M. Länsiluoto, A. Partanen, V. Pellinen, J. (2013). *Talousohjaus ja kustannuslaskenta*. Sanoma Pro Oy.

➢ Jiwa, Z. Siagan, H. Jie, F. (2020). The Role of Top Management Commitment to Enhancing the Competitive Advantage Through ERP Integration and Purchasing Strategy. *ResearchGate*. https://www.researchgate.net/publication/338319328_The_Role_of_Top_Management_Commitment_to_Enhancing_the_Competitive_Advantage_Through_ERP_Integration_and__Purchasing_Strategy

➢ GrowEQ. (2023). *The Importance of Management Commitment*. https://www.groweq.com.au/the-importance-of-management-commitment/

➢ Robbins, S.P. & Judge, T.A. (2022). *Essentials of Organizational Behavior*. Pearson Education Limited.

➢ Ignition. (2024). *KPIs for Product Managers: total cost of ownership*. https://www.haveignition.com/kpis-for-product-managers/kpis-for-product-managers-total-cost-of-ownership

➢ Centre of Industrial Management-Katholieke Universiteit Leuven. (Year unknown). *Individual Assignment of Advanced Management Accounting*. http://handik_w.tripod.com/sitebuildercontent/sitebuilderfiles/tco.pdf

➢ Gartner. (2024). *Cost Structure*. https://www.gartner.com/en/finance/glossary/cost-structure

➢ Berger, B. (2.12.2011). Spending Cuts without the Cheese Slicer! *IFM PFM BLOG – Public Financial Management*. https://blog-pfm.imf.org/en/pfmblog/2011/12/spending-cuts-without-the-cheese-slicer

➢ Gartner. (2024). *Use Total Cost of Ownership to Optimize Costs and Increase Savings*. https://www.gartner.com/en/documents/3847267

➢ Schmidt, J. (2015 – 2024). Cost Structure – The different types of cost structures incurred by a business. *CFI Education Inc*. https://corporatefinanceinstitute.com/resources/accounting/cost-structure/

➢ Indeed Editorial Team. (16.8.2024). The Types of Costing in Cost Accounting. *Indeed – Career development*. https://www.indeed.com/career-advice/career-development/types-of-costing

➢ Kagan, J. (30.7.2024). Payback Period: Definition, Formula, and Calculation. *Investopedia.* https://www.investopedia.com/terms/p/paybackperiod.asp

➢ Hayes, A. (17.4.2024). Cash Flow: What It Is, How It Works, and How to Analyze It. *Investopedia.* https://www.investopedia.com/terms/c/cashflow.asp

➢ Jansson, C. (2018). Financial Resilience: The Role of Financial Balance, Profitability, and Ownership. *The Resilience Framework*, 111–131. https://www.researchgate.net/publication/319449764_Financial_Resilience_The_Role_of_Financial_Balance_Profitability_and_Ownership

➢ Eurostat. (2024). Industrial producer price index overview**.** *Eurostat – Statistics Explained*. https://ec.europa.eu/eurostat/statistics-explained/index.php?title=Industrial_producer_price_index_overview#Industrial_producer_prices_-_development_since_2015

➢ Hermarij, J. (2021). *Better Practices of Project Management – 4th fully revised edition. Based on IPMA Competences – ICB Version 4.* Van Haren Publishing.

➢ ProjectManager.com. (2024). *Project Scheduling: How to Make a Schedule.* https://www.projectmanager.com/guides/project-scheduling

➢ Andriani, R., Disman, D. (2023). Effects of work overload and job stress on employee performance: categorical moderation from poly-chronicity and work environment. *JPPI (Journal Penelitian Pendidikan Indonesia).* https://www.researchgate.net/publication/376496148_Effects_Of_Work_Overload_and_Job_Stress_on_Employee_Performance_Categorical_Moderation_from_Polychronicity_and_Work_Environment

➢ Ranganath, R. (2.7.2024). Effective Cost Control in Construction Projects. *ProQsmart.* https://proqsmart.com/blog/cost-control-in-construction/

➢ Ruslanova, D. (2024). Definition of Project kickoff meeting. *Maddevs.io*. https://maddevs.io/glossary/project-kickoff-meeting/

➢ Crane, A., Matten, D., Glozer, S., Spence, L. (2019). *Business Ethics – Fifth edition.* Oxford University Press.

➢ Browaeys, M.-J. & Price, R. (2019). *Understanding Cross-Cultural Management.* Pearson Education Limited.

➢ Mujtaba, B.G. (2008). Task and Relationship Orientations of Thai and American Business Students based on Cultural Contexts Introduction and Cultural Values. *Journal of Leadership Education.* https://www-emerald-com.proxy.uwasa.fi/insight/content/doi/10.12806/V18/I2/R8/full/pdf?title=projectmanage rleadershipbehaviortask-oriented-versus-relationship-oriented

➢ Indeed Editorial Team. (16.8.2024). The Importance of Resource Management (With 10 Benefits). *Indeed – Career development*. https://www.indeed.com/career-advice/career-development/resource-management-importance

➢ Lastiri, L. (22.9.2023). 5 Tips for Streamlining Data Analysis and Reporting for Actionable Insights. *Kippy*. https://www.kippy.cloud/post/tips-for-streamlining-data-analysis-and-reporting-for-actionable-insights

➢ Eleya, J. (28.6.2023). 6 Benefits of a Good Management Reporting System. *Envisio*. https://envisio.com/blog/6-benefits-of-a-good-management-reporting-system/

➢ Bridges, J. (3.5.2023). Project Coordinator Job Description: Role, Responsibilities & Skills. *ProjectManager*. https://www.projectmanager.com/training/role-project-coordinator

➢ Indeed Editorial Team. (16.8.2024). What Is Project Coordination and How Does It Work? *Indeed – Career development*. https://www.indeed.com/career-advice/career-development/coordinating-projects

➢ Fatma, A. & Kumar, M. (2024). Exploring the Correlation Between Service Quality and Customer Satisfaction in the Hospitality Industry. *The International Journal of Indian Psychology*. https://www.researchgate.net/publication/378711872_Exploring_the_Correlation_Between_Service_Quality_and_Customer_Satisfaction_in_the_Hospitality_Industry

➢ PanLearn. (2024). *Benefits of Project Documentation*. https://www.panlearn.com/articles/project-management/get-project-management-experience-for-pmp-certification

➢ Law Insider. (2013 – 2024). *Engineering Data Definition*. https://www.lawinsider.com/dictionary/engineering-data

➢ Hawker, M. (12.5.2023). 5 Ways Bad Data Hurts Your Business [and How to Fix It]. *Profisee*. https://profisee.com/blog/5-ways-bad-data-hurts-business/

➢ Fowler, P. (19.6.2019). The "Definition of Quality". *Pete Fowler Construction Services, Inc*. https://www.petefowler.com/blog/2019/6/19/the-definition-of-quality

➢ Hussain, S.S. (13.10.2023). What are the 4 key components of quality management? *LinkedIn*. https://www.linkedin.com/pulse/what-4-key-components-quality-management-saleem-sarwar-hussain/

➢ Indeed Editorial Team. (5.9.2023). *What is quality planning? (Definition and importance).* https://uk.indeed.com/career-advice/career-development/quality-planning

➢ Gillis, A. S. (2024). What is quality assurance (QA)? *TechTarget.* https://www.techtarget.com/searchsoftwarequality/definition/quality-assurance

➢ International Organization for Standardization. (Year unknown). *Quality assurance: A critical ingredient for organizational success.* https://www.iso.org/quality-management/quality-assurance

➢ Indeed Editorial Team. (23.1.2024). *What Is Quality Control? Definition, Importance and Methods.* https://www.indeed.com/career-advice/career-development/what-is-quality-control

➢ ComplianceOnline. (2024). *ISO 31000 and Enterprise Risk Management.* https://www.complianceonline.com/dictionary/ISO_31000_Enterprise_Risk_Management.html

➢ Hessing, T. (Year unknown). Cost of Poor Quality (COPQ). *Sixsigmastudyguide.com.* https://sixsigmastudyguide.com/cost-of-poor-quality/

➢ SSDSI. (22.12.2023). *Cost of Poor Quality (COPQ).* https://sixsigmadsi.com/copq-what-does-it-mean/

➢ Whittington, R., Regnér, P., Angwin, D., Johnson, G. Scholes, K. (2020). *Exploring Strategy – Twelfth Edition.* Pearson Education Limited.

➢ Kaplan, R. & Norton, D. (2004). *Strategiakartat (Strategy Maps).* Talentum Oy, original English version published by arrangement with Harvard Business School Press.

➢ Investopedia. (17.10.2024). *Funding Available for Companies?* Date accessed 21.10.2024. Retrieved from web site URL https://www.investopedia.com/ask/answers/03/062003.asp

➢ Hayes, A. (4.9.2024). Revenue Definition, Formula, Calculation, and Examples. *Investopedia.* https://www.investopedia.com/terms/r/revenue.asp

➢ 4cost GmbH (2008 – 2024). *Should Cost Analysis: Benefits and Use Cases.* https://www.4cost.de/en/resources/blog/should-cost-analysis-2/

➢ Herrera Piscopo, G., Johnston, W. and Bellenger, D.N. (2008), Total cost of ownership and customer value in business markets" Woodside, A.G., Golfetto, F. and Gibbert, M. (Ed.) Creating and managing superior customer value (Advances in Business Marketing and Purchasing, Vol. 14), Emerald Group Publishing Limited, Leeds, pp. 205-220. https://doi.org/10.1016/S1069-0964(08)14006-6

➢ Your company formations. (2024). *Guide to Company Shareholders.*
https://www.yourcompanyformations.co.uk/learning-centre/company-shareholders/

➢ MBB Management. (29.12.2023). What is the Role of the Standard Business Owner?
MBB Production, LLC. https://www.mbbmanagement.com/business-management/what-is-the-role-of-the-standard-business-owner/

➢ Ontario Securities Commission. (2024). *Factors that can affect stock prices.*
https://www.getsmarteraboutmoney.ca/learning-path/stocks/factors-that-can-affect-stock-prices/

➢ Kagan, J. (9.3.2024). Credit Rating: Definition and Importance to Investors. *Investopedia.*
https://www.investopedia.com/terms/c/creditrating.asp

➢ Alternative Business Funding. (2024). *How your Credit Score Can Impact Your Business Finance.* https://www.alternativebusinessfunding.co.uk/knowledge/growing-fast/how-your-credit-score-can-impact-your-business-finance/

➢ Hoffman, R.R., Zachary, W., Burns, J. Drillings, M., Hale, C. R., Linegang, M. (2008). Human total cost of ownership: Measuring the impact of human factors in system engineering. *Proceedings of the Human Factors and Ergonomics Society Annual Meeting* *52*(4), 202–205.
https://www.researchgate.net/publication/274977029_Human_Total_Cost_of_Ownership_Measuring_the_Impact_of_Human_Factors_on_System_Engineering

➢ xe currency converter. (23.10.2024). *2,250,000 USD to EUR - Convert US Dollars to Euros.*
https://www.xe.com/currencyconverter/convert/?Amount=2250000&From=USD&To=EUR

➢ Herrity, J. (18.9.2024). Maslow's Hierarchy of Needs: Applying It in the Workplace. *Indeed – Career Development.* https://www.indeed.com/career-advice/career-development/maslows-hierarchy-of-needs

➢ Knight, R. (13.12.2023). 8 Essential Qualities of Successful Leaders. *Harvard Business Review.* https://hbr.org/2023/12/8-essential-qualities-of-successful-leaders

➢ Merriam-Webster. (2024). *Commitment.* https://www.merriam-webster.com/dictionary/commitment

➢ Armstrong, M. & Murlis, H. (2007). *Reward Management – A Handbook of Renumeration Strategy and Practice.* Kogan Page Limited.
https://books.google.fi/books?hl=fi&lr=&id=oTaSWA-

FeroC&oi=fnd&pg=PR8&dq=guiding+organisational+behaviour+with+wage+and+reward
ing&ots=INmfGBAZ71&sig=7nRkNIDmzG7B1ud1pR3ck8x_MHs&redir_esc=y#v=onepage
&q=guiding%20organisational%20behaviour%20with%20wage%20and%20rewarding&f=
false

➢ Säkkinen, Hannu. (2024). *Neuvottelutaidot tulevaisuuden menestyksen takaajina (Negotiation skills guaranteeing the future success).* Lecture in the Project Days 2024, Helsinki, Finland.

➢ Dwesini, N. F. (2019). Causes and prevention of high employee turnover within the hospitality industry: A literature review. *African Journal of Hospitality, Tourism and Leisure 8*(3), 1–14. https://core.ac.uk/download/pdf/200897091.pdf

➢ Shweta. (3.6.2024). Employee Turnover Rate: Definition & Calculation. *Forber Advisor.* https://www.forbes.com/advisor/business/employee-turnover-rate/

➢ Montañez, R. (22.3.2024). Fighting Loneliness on Remote Teams. https://hbr.org/2024/03/fighting-loneliness-on-remote-teams

➢ Ross, I. C. & Zander, A. (1957). Need Satisfactions and Employee Turnover. *Personnel Psychology 10*(3), 327–338. https://onlinelibrary.wiley.com/doi/abs/10.1111/j.1744-6570.1957.tb00786.x

➢ Cagnassola, M. E. (14.9.2022). Working at the Office Costs Twice as Much as Working Remote: Survey. *Money.* https://money.com/working-office-vs-working-remote-costs/

➢ Gibbs, M., Mengel, F. & Siemroth, C. (2023). Work from Home and Productivity: Evidence from Personnel and Analytics Data on Information Technology Professionals. *Journal of Political Economy Microeconomics 1*(1), 1-224. https://www.journals.uchicago.edu/doi/epdf/10.1086/721803

➢ Kenton, W. (24.11.2020). Silo Mentality: Definition in Business, Causes, and Solutions. *Investopedia.* https://www.investopedia.com/terms/s/silo-mentality.asp

➢ Mouta, C. & Meneses, R. (2021). The impact of CEO characteristics on organizational culture and on the silo effect. *Revista Brasileira de Gestão de Negocios, 23*(2), 205-227. https://doi.org/10.7819/rbgn.v23i2.4100

➢ Lipkin, N. (25.10.2022). Our brains want to be lazy; here's how to win the battle. *Forbes.* https://www.forbes.com/sites/nicolelipkin/2022/10/25/our-brains-want-to-be-lazy-heres-how-to-win-the-battle/

➢ Halton, C. (26.5.2024). Downsizing: Meaning, Consequences, and Examples. *Investopedia.* https://www.investopedia.com/terms/d/downsize.asp

➢ Strunk, K. O., Goldhaber, D, Knight, D. S. & Brown, N. (2018). Are There Hidden Costs Associated with Conducting Layoffs? The Impact of Reduction-in-Force and Layoff

Notices on Teacher Effectiveness. *Journal of Policy Analysis and Management, 37*(4), 755-782. https://doi.org/10.1002/pam.22074

➢ Brookman, J. T., Chang, S. & Rennie, G. G. (2007). CEO Cash and Stock-Based Compensation Changes, Layoff Decisions, and Shareholder Value. *The Financial Review 42*(1), 99-119. https://onlinelibrary.wiley.com/doi/epdf/10.1111/j.1540-6288.2007.00163.x

➢ Kennemer, K. (17.11.2016). 5 Reasons for a No Layoff Policy. *LinkedIn.* https://www.linkedin.com/pulse/5-reasons-layoff-policy-kevin-kennemer/

➢ xe.com. (1.11.2024). *490,000,000 INR to EUR - Convert Indian Rupees to Euros.* https://www.xe.com/currencyconverter/convert/?Amount=490000000&From=INR&To=EUR

➢ xe.com. (1.11.2024). *1,440,000,000 INR to EUR - Convert Indian Rupees to Euros.* https://www.xe.com/currencyconverter/convert/?Amount=1440000000&From=INR&To=EUR

➢ Business Today. (3.1.2024). *Zero layoff strategy: The secret to Appinventiv's growth during the 2023 recession.* https://www.businesstoday.in/impact-feature/story/zero-layoff-strategy-the-secret-to-appinventivs-growth-during-the-2023-recession-411730-2024-01-03

➢ Sinek, S. (2019). *Leaders Eat Last – Why Some Teams Pull Together and Others Don't.* Penguin Business.

➢ Shields, R. (17.7.2023). The Real Costs of Recruitment. *LinkedIn.* https://www.linkedin.com/pulse/real-costs-recruitment-rebekah-shields/

➢ Indeed Editorial Team. (16.8.2024). *What Does the Research and Development Department Do?* https://www.indeed.com/career-advice/career-development/what-does-the-research-and-development-department-do

➢ Noble, C. H. & Kumar, M. (2010). Exploring the Appeal of Product Design: A Grounded, Value-Based Model of Key Design Elements and Relationships. *Journal of Product Innovation Management, 27*(5), 640-657. https://onlinelibrary.wiley.com/doi/abs/10.1111/j.1540-5885.2010.00742.x

➢ Seasia Infotech. (26.5.2022). *What Are the 10 Stages in the New Product Development Process?* https://www.seasiainfotech.com/blog/everything-about-new-product-development/

➢ Marion, T. J. & Meyer, M. H. (2011). Applying Industrial Design and Cost Engineering to New Product Development in Early-Stage Firms. *Journal of Product Innovation Management, 28*(5), 773-786. https://onlinelibrary.wiley.com/doi/10.1111/j.1540-5885.2011.00839.x

➤ Feil, P., Keun-Hyo, Y. & Il-Woon, K. (2004). Japanese Target Costing: A Historical Perspective. *International Journal of Strategic Cost Management (Spring),* 10-19. http://scsol.co.kr/img/sc/bufile/japanese%20target%20costing.pdf

➤ Tasdeviren, G. (8.11.2016). What is Genka kikaku (Target cost) and how it works? *Linked*In. https://www.linkedin.com/pulse/what-genka-kikaku-target-cost-how-works-gokhan-tasdeviren/

➤ Ibusuki, U. & Kaminski, P. C. (2007). Product development process with focus on value engineering and target-costing: A case study in an automotive company. *International Journal of Production Economics 105*(2), 459-474. https://www-sciencedirect-com.proxy.uwasa.fi/science/article/pii/S0925527306000958

➤ Hinshaw, M. (3.1.2023). What is Design to Value vs. Design to Cost? *aPriori*. https://www.apriori.com/blog/what-is-design-to-value-vs-design-to-cost/

➤ Kowalczyk, D. (18.7.2024). Special Characteristics and their identification in new project implementation. *Automotive Quality Solutions*. https://www.automotivequal.com/special-characteristics-and-their-identification-during-new-project-implementation/

➤ Gepard. (2024). What Is Product Variant? What Is Product Variant?

➤ Engineering Product Design. (2024). *Design for Manufacture and Assembly (DfMA)*. https://engineeringproductdesign.com/knowledge-base/design-for-manufacture-and-assembly/

➤ Wikipedia. (3.9.2023). *Concurrent engineering*. https://en.wikipedia.org/wiki/Concurrent_engineering

➤ Syan, C. S. & Menon, U. (1994). *Concurrent Engineering: Concepts, implementation and practice.* Springer-Science+Business Media, B.V.

➤ Oboloo. (26.5.2023). Maximizing Efficiency: The Benefits of Simultaneous Engineering. *Oboloo*. https://oboloo.com/maximizing-efficiency-the-benefits-of-simultaneous-engineering/

➤ Meadows Analysis & Design, LLC. (8.11.2018). *Concurrent Engineering: What Is It and What Benefits Does It Offer?* https://meadowsanalysis.com/concurrent-engineering-what-is-it-and-what-benefits-does-it-offer/

➤ Marcetic, N. (5.6.2022). Value Added vs Non Value Added Activities. *Lean Community*. https://leancommunity.org/value-added-vs-non-value-added/

➤ The Finnish Industrial Union. (2020). *Työntutkimuksen käsitteitä, menettelytapoja ja käyttökohteita*. https://www.teollisuusliitto.fi/wp-content/uploads/2020/05/200507_Tyotutkimus.pdf

➤ Malsam, W. (26.9.2023). Manufacturing Engineer Job Description. *ProjectManager*. https://www.projectmanager.com/blog/manufacturing-engineering

➤ Indeed Editorial Team. (29.4.2024). What Is a Process Engineer? A Complete Guide. *Indeed – Career Guide*. https://in.indeed.com/career-advice/finding-a-job/what-is-a-process-engineer

➤ Dr. Veena, C. (2019). Ergonomics and employee engagement. *International Journal of Mechanical Engineering and Technology 10*(2), 105-109. https://d1wqtxts1xzle7.cloudfront.net/58953939/IJMET_10_02_01320190419-33807-k53ler-libre.pdf?1555672971=&response-content-disposition=inline%3B+filename%3DERGONOMICS_AND_EMPLOYEE_ENGAGEMENT.pdf&Expires=1731758390&Signature=hCFO-2r8SvR-MlnH9Bkh4C4sLFkQiDjIomdNKR8XVM8Pc19Gg8-aDiv2xjp9Q3Kkav81ydgNBgzz2ZOZlMJRn7m1JfSjZd7wvmAwBiNQiaQdsoBm0gYoIShL2XAfrZVNLyAWUYEwJBnJxDpcAi64TMIkQi91wsSIfaXni0MGUvu7h2N5NUIi0aFuInp~ZUWERrYqylDVBopzrrDTV50qHGcVKaZy9t2vE9zt1rd5zNAF32qCF~ZVuTGn-Kr~XOQWgaM~Embg4VK91LjHAs2RTuyigHrDtlm4ov9gqE-CaEurLv5UwGMxczp0FWYSuhZhPRJedyAnB2Feom5GK8NdzA__&Key-Pair-Id=APKAJLOHF5GGSLRBV4ZA

➤ Hayes, A. (24.7.2024). What Is Throughput? Definition, Formula, Benefits, and Calculation. *Investopedia*. https://www.investopedia.com/terms/t/throughput.asp

➤ Worximity. (25.4.2024). *How to Analyze Throughput Rate*. https://www.worximity.com/blog/analyzing-throughput-rate

➤ OEE. (2024). *Overall Equipment Effectiveness*. https://www.oee.com/

➤ Physiopedia. (2024). *Gait Definitions*. https://www.physio-pedia.com/Gait_Definitions

➤ Motin Controls Robotics. (2024). *Robot Inertia vs Payload*. https://motioncontrolsrobotics.com/resources/tech-talk-articles/robot-inertia-vs-payload/

➤ Floyd, T. (15.12.2021). What Is Karakuri? *Geolean*. https://geoleanusa.com/what-is-karakuri/

➤ Daniel, D. (2021). Kaizen (continuous improvement). *TechTarget*. https://www.techtarget.com/searcherp/definition/kaizen-or-continuous-improvement

➤ Reid, H. (6.6.2023). What is First in First Out (FIFO)? Definition, Pros and Cons. *DCL Logistics*. https://dclcorp.com/blog/inventory/fifo/

➤ Fernando, J. (27.6.2024). Supply Chain Management (SCM): How It Works & Why It's Important. *Investopedia*. https://www.investopedia.com/terms/s/scm.asp

➤ Caniato, F., Ronchi, S., Luzzini, D. & Brivio, O. (2015). Total cost of ownership along the supply chain: a model applied to the tinting industry. *Production Planning & Control –*

The Management of Operations. https://doi-org.proxy.uwasa.fi/10.1080/09537287.2014.918285

➤ Oskarsson, B. (2019). *Total Cost Analysis in Logistics - Practical Execution, Learning, and Teaching in Higher Education.* Linköping Studies in Science and Technology, Dissertations, No. 2032. https://www.diva-portal.org/smash/get/diva2:1367153/FULLTEXT01.pdf

➤ Sunny, B. (14.2.2023). Benefits of Total Cost of Ownership (TCO) Analysis in Supply Chain Management. *Medium.* https://sunnysimbiam.medium.com/the-benefits-of-tco-analysis-in-supply-chain-management-41f65838dfb9

➤ Schönsleben, Prof. em. Dr. Paul. (Year unknown). Integral Logistics Management — Operations Management and Supply Chain Management Within and Across Companies. *Opess ETH Zurich.* https://opess.ethz.ch/course/section-2-1/2-1-3-total-cost-of-ownership-in-a-global-supply-chain/

➤ The Sourcing Co. (Year Unknown). *What is Supplier Management? A Comprehensive Guide.* https://thesourcing.co/what-is-supplier-management

➤ Everything Supply Chain. (2024). *Supplier Management Strategies for the Lowest Total Cost of Ownership (TCO).* https://www.everythingsupplychain.com/supplier-management-strategies-for-the-lowest-total-cost-of-ownership-tco/

➤ Carvajal, A. (24.4.2023). What Does the Supplier Contract Management Process Look Like? *Top.legal.* https://www.top.legal/en/knowledge/supplier-contract-management-process

➤ Nysten-Haarala, S., Hirvonen-Ere, S. & Ketola, A. (18.9.2024). Miten ratkaista suurten yhteisprojektien ja niiden innovaatioiden muutos- ja ongelmatilanteita? (How to solve change and problem situations in big collaborative projects and concerning the innovations in them?). Panel discussion in the Project Days Helsinki, 2024.

➤ Logistiikan Maailma. (2024). *Inbound, Intra and Outbound logistics.* https://www.logistiikanmaailma.fi/en/logistics/logistics-and-supply-chain/inbound-inhouse-and-outbound-logistics/

➤ Barrios, K. (27.9.2021). A Full Breakdown of Incoterms (International Commercial Terms). *Xeneta.* https://www.xeneta.com/blog/incoterms

➤ International Trade Administration. (Year unknown). *Know Your Incoterms.* https://www.trade.gov/know-your-incoterms

➢ IPQC. (19.4.2022). *What is Incoming Quality Control – IQC Inspection Definition, Importance, Methods and More*. https://www.ipqcco.com/blog/what-is-incoming-quality-control-iqc-inspection-definition-importance-methods-and-more

➢ Shuler, K. (5.9.2021). What's the Difference Between Sourcing, Purchasing, and Procurement? *Quandary Consulting Group*. https://quandarycg.com/difference-between-sourcing-purchasing-and-procurement/

➢ Forsten-Astikainen, R., Hurmelinna-Laukkanen, P., Lämsä, T., Heilmann, P., Hyrkäs, E. (2017). Dealing with organizational silos with communities of practice and human resource management. *Journal of Workplace Learning 29*(6), 473-489. https://doi.org/10.1108/JWL-04-2015-0028

➢ University of Michigan. (2024). *Career Path Navigator - Production Planning and Control Manager*. https://careernavigator.umich.edu/job_detail/102746/production-planning-and-control-manager

➢ Bika, N. (3.2.2020). Materials Manager job description. *Workable*. https://resources.workable.com/materials-manager-job-description

➢ Blink. (6.9.2023). *How to build and structure your internal communications team*. https://www.joinblink.com/intelligence/internal-communications-team

➢ Hudson, P. T. W. & Stephens, D. (2000). *Cost and Benefit in HSE: A Model for Calculation of Cost-Benefit using Incident Potential*. Paper presented at the SPE International Conference on Health, Safety and Environment in Oil and Gas Exploration and Production, Stavanger, Norway, June 2000. https://doi.org/10.2118/61050-MS

➢ Brosschot, J. F., Verkuil, B. & Thayer, J. F. (2018). Generalized Unsafety Theory of Stress: Unsafe Environments and Conditions, and the Default Stress Response. *International Journal of Environmental Research and Public Health 15*(3), 464. https://doi.org/10.3390/ijerph15030464

➢ Indeed Editorial Team. (9.3.2024). What Is an HSE Manager? (With Duties, How-to, and Skills). *Indeed – Career Guide*. https://ca.indeed.com/career-advice/finding-a-job/what-is-hse-manager

➢ Water Power Technologies Office. (Year unknown). Environment, Health, and Safety Professional. *Office of Energy Efficiency & Renewable Energy*. https://www.energy.gov/eere/water/environment-health-and-safety-professional-0

➢ EcoOnline. (Year unknown). *Health, Safety, and Environment (HSE)*. https://www.ecoonline.com/glossary/health-safety-and-environment

➢ Sink, R. (17.8.2017). The Insider's Guide to Total Cost of Ownership. *Deringer*. https://blog.anderinger.com/blog/the-insiders-guide-to-total-cost-of-ownership

- Sheldon, R. (Year unknown). HVAC (heating, ventilation and air conditioning). *TechTarget.* https://www.techtarget.com/searchdatacenter/definition/HVAC
- NLR. (2024). *Mould Exposure: Long Term Side Effects.* https://nlr.com.au/articles/mould-exposure-long-term-side-effects

© 2025 Petri S. Nieminen

Publisher: BoD · Books on Demand, Mannerheimintie 12 B,

00100 Helsinki, bod@bod.fi

Print: Libri Plureos GmbH, Friedensallee 273,

22763 Hampuri, Saksa

ISBN: 978-952-80-8575-1